What people are saying about Zest.[1]

'I would imagine the authors approached some heavyweight "names" to recommend this book but that they were turned down. Proper authors – Simon Singh, Deepak Chopra – people like that. I wouldn't put it past the authors to just make up a whole load of stupid comments and stick them in. I mean, how ridiculous would that be?'

Mr Right, Isle of Write

'I've built my career and fortune on making the subject of personal development detailed and overly complex. We can't have simplicity like this within the genre, it will ruin many careers. Please do not publish!'

Anne Academic, Cambridge

'*Zest* – what a shit title. If I want "zest" I'll buy a fucking lemon.'

Richard Head, Braintree

'Too many pithy quotes and gags for me. I mean, since when did self-help become entertaining?'

Lucy Fer, Strasbourg

'Who the hell's got time to read a book these days?'

Justin Time, Bolton

'I understand the concepts but, quite frankly, they're not for me. If I start smiling at work, they'll think I'm on something.'

Helen Hywater, Banbury

'Who let these idiots loose with a laptop? This book is proof that the gene pool needs chlorinating.'

Kirsten Swore, Wolverhampton

'"You can put your boots in the oven but that don't make them biscuits." I've got no idea what that quote means so I was delighted it didn't appear in this book. Well done authors.'

Miles A. Head, Newport

'This book is too thin to be any good and the cover is overly bright. The quality of a personal development book is measured by weight and the seriousness of the cover. It certainly shouldn't be fun and easy to read. What were the authors thinking?'

A. Pompoustwat, Athens

'This book is fab. Awaken the *Zest* within.'

Tony Robbins, Bexhill-on-Sea

---

[1] *Probably?*

ZEST

ZEST

How to Squeeze the Max out of Life

Andy Cope, Gavin Oattes, Will Hussey
Illustrations by Amy Bradley

CAPSTONE
A Wiley Brand

This edition first published 2019

© 2019 Andy Cope, Gavin Oattes, Will Hussey and Amy Bradley

Registered office
John Wiley & Sons Ltd, The Atrium, Southern Gate, Chichester, West Sussex, PO19 8SQ, United Kingdom

For details of our global editorial offices, for customer services and for information about how to apply for permission to reuse the copyright material in this book please see our website at www.wiley.com.

Wiley publishes in a variety of print and electronic formats and by print-on-demand. Some material included with standard print versions of this book may not be included in e-books or in print-on-demand. If this book refers to media such as a CD or DVD that is not included in the version you purchased, you may download this material at http://booksupport.wiley.com. For more information about Wiley products, visit www.wiley.com.

Designations used by companies to distinguish their products are often claimed as trademarks. All brand names and product names used in this book are trade names, service marks, trademarks or registered trademarks of their respective owners. The publisher is not associated with any product or vendor mentioned in this book.

Limit of Liability/Disclaimer of Warranty: While the publisher and author have used their best efforts in preparing this book, they make no representations or warranties with respect to the accuracy or completeness of the contents of this book and specifically disclaim any implied warranties of merchantability or fitness for a particular purpose. It is sold on the understanding that the publisher is not engaged in rendering professional services and neither the publisher nor the author shall be liable for damages arising herefrom. If professional advice or other expert assistance is required, the services of a competent professional should be sought.

Library of Congress Cataloging-in-Publication Data

Names: Cope, Andrew, author. | Oattes, Gavin, author. | Hussey, Will, author.
Title: Zest : how to squeeze the max out of life / Andy Cope, Gavin Oattes, Will Hussey.
Description: First Edition. | Hoboken : Capstone, 2019. | Includes index. |
  Identifiers: LCCN 2019014817 (print) | LCCN 2019017024 (ebook) | ISBN
  9780857088062 (Adobe PDF) | ISBN 9780857088031 (ePub) | ISBN 9780857088000
  (paperback) | ISBN 9780857088062 (ePDF)
Subjects: LCSH: Self-actualization (Psychology) | Self-confidence | BISAC:
  SELF-HELP / General.
Classification: LCC BF637.S4 (ebook) | LCC BF637.S4 C66477 2019 (print) | DDC
  158.1—dc23
LC record available at https://lccn.loc.gov/2019014817

A catalogue record for this book is available from the British Library.

ISBN 978-0-857-08800-0 (paperback) ISBN 978-0-857-08806-2 (ePDF)
ISBN 978-0-857-08803-1 (ePub)

10 9 8 7 6 5 4 3 2 1

Cover Design: Wiley
Cover Image: © Amy Bradley

Set in 10/14pt Frutiger LT Std by Aptara, New Delhi, India

Printed in Great Britain by Bell & Bain Ltd, Glasgow

It's said that behind every successful man there's a woman, rolling her eyes. In our case, that'll be Helen, Ali and Lou.

Thank you.

Thank you.

And thank you.

CONTENTS

Part 1

YOU 2.0 (THE RE-BOOT)

A Word about Threesomes

Three authors? That's weird.

Three's a crowd, not a team. And the modern world has introduced us to the 'threesome'. We're good friends but we're not *that* good!

> 'I believe that no matter how random things may appear, there's still a plan.'
>
> *Col. John 'Hannibal' Smith*
> *(The A-Team)*

We're buoyed by the fact there were 3 Musketeers, 3 Wise Men and 3 Stooges. Charlie had 3 Angels. And a single Bananarama would just be … *well* … a banana.

So although 3 can be a crowd, it can also be Amigos, and that's us. Yes, dear reader, we are your Harry, Ron and Hermione; Snap, Crackle and Pop, and your blind mice.

We all bring different things to the table. Dr Andy's an established author. A proper old timer with serious literary miles on his clock. If you're a loyal reader of his fabled back catalogue, guess what, those themes will reappear. Unrelenting and unapologetic, this is no house built on sand. Andy's science gives *Zest* a solid foundation – 15 years of rock solid academia – for Gav and Will to build on. Think 'same but different'.

Will? He was a teacher and now champions learning. Anywhere and everywhere. With everyone and anyone. He's the best writer of the three by a million miles. His prose is silky, almost to the point of sensual. Will waxes (lyrically, not Brazilianally). You'll know when Will's writing cos you'll be feeling a tinge of arousal.

And that leaves Gav. He's an original. A comic first and foremost but there's a difference between being stand-up funny and page-turningly funny. He writes in short sharp bursts. He's a bit sweary so there's a balance between letting him loose and reining him in – just a smidge. Gav doesn't wax. He just tells it as it is in all its hairy glory. This book is peppered with #Gavisms. Think of them as short sharp no-nonsense wake-up calls, the literary equivalent of an ECG.

Electrodes attached, power charged, stand back – *BZZZZZT.*

So that's us. The good, the bad and the ugly, here to prove that threesomes can be wholesome.

But *Zest* isn't about us. So it's over to you …

Are you sitting comfortably?

Before we begin properly, we thought we'd set the scene. So here's a story that sums up the entire book. It's a story about a story. A story about a story, that happens to be a *true* story.

Rewind to Gav's teacher training days. He's 20 years old, knows next to nothing and is doing a placement at a primary school. He's sitting in the staffroom, fish out of water, waiting to be allocated a class to go and observe …

My mentor gave me the nod. 'Nursery,' she said. 'And rather than just watching, wouldn't it be great if we got you involved.' She must have seen the panic in my eyes. 'It's the very best way to learn,' she reassured, before turning on her heels and flouncing down the corridor.

I had no choice but to fall in line and flounce behind, hoping she couldn't hear the screaming in my head. *The bloody nursery? I wanna be a teacher not a Lego builder.* I didn't know much but I knew this much – nurseries are just big rooms full of 3 and 4-year-olds, mini Oompa Loompas, running and eating. They eat when they're running and run while they're eating. Even when they're not running and eating, in their minds they're running and eating. *And 'get involved'? What does she mean, 'get involved'?*

The nursery was as imagined, a seething mass of hyperactivity, Lego and dinosaurs. The teacher turned to me and told me that she would like me to pick a book and read it to the class. I did a double take. *What? Me? Reading a story? To 40 Oompa Loompas?*

5

My heart raced as she herded the tiny human beings into the reading corner. *Gulp! My first test!* Thankfully, on the top shelf was my favourite book of all time, *The Very Hungry Caterpillar*. I realized this was my big chance to win the kids over.

I sat on the big chair, you know the one.

The children were sitting wide-eyed and waiting, their excitement piqued by never having seen a male teacher before. They were cross-legged, except for the ones who couldn't. You might be one of those ones. The ones who can't cross their legs. But we're still made to cross our legs. I am one of those ones. I used to have to snap my legs into place.

Every child sat and looked at me with their best face – do it now for me please, so you can remember the face I'm talking about – a mix of anticipation, love, Christmas Eve and awe. If you're reading this book in bed or on the train, tap the person next to you on the shoulder and show them your 'best face'. Your '4-year-old-about-to-be-read-a-story-to face'.

I took a deep breath and began to read the book. After the first couple of pages I thought I'd have a quick look up just to make sure the kids were okay. As I lifted my head I realized something strange had happened. Every single child appeared to have moved closer.

I carried on reading. Another couple of pages and again I looked up, every single child was even closer. Or were they? Was I imagining things or were they Dr Who's weeping angels?

Don't blink Gavin. DO. NOT. BLINK!

I decided to try and catch them out. I looked down but immediately looked back up again. I caught them! Every single one of them on their bums moving forward like a wee army of ants – they were killer ants, coming to attack me.

Keep reading the book, keep reading the book, I told myself.

One tiny boy began to take my shoe off.

I was aware that my mentor was watching. Her tick sheet was out. She was grading me! *Keep reading the book, keep reading the book.*

From the corner of my eye I could see my shoe being passed all the way to the back of the class.

Keep reading the book, keep reading the book.

In my peripheral vision I could see my shoe being passed along the back row. One little boy was flying my shoe, the next was chatting into it like a phone and one even licked my shoe. *WHY? Why would you lick a shoe?* All I could think was *keep reading the book, keep reading the book*, that's what I had been asked to do. 'On Thursday he ate through *fouuuur* strawberries, but he was *stiiiill* hungry …'

My shoe was now on its way back. From the corner of my eye, I could see it being passed forward from child to child. It finally reached the front row, made its way back to the same child who removed it in the first place and like Cinderella's prince, he simply popped my shoe back onto my foot and loudly stated for all to hear, 'I'VE GOT TWO SHOES!'

I learned in that moment exactly what happens when a 4-year-old publicly announces how many shoes he/she has.

EVERYONE publicly announces how many shoes they have! And guess what? All forty of them also have two shoes!

All of a sudden, amidst the global announcement of how many shoes everyone is wearing, things moved up a gear. Another small child began to climb my leg. Now, when I say 'climb', I mean climbing, actual climbing. I'm certain this kid was wearing a rucksack. And carried a map. And a compass (I'm not sure if this part is true or if I made it up but I hope it is).

So, picture the scene. I'm now sitting in front of the whole class and there's a small boy sitting on my leg just staring at my face. I tried to ignore him, I'm a professional, right? But we were almost nose-to-nose. So I turned and said, 'Can I help you?'

'I just really wanna see the pictures,' he replied.

And that's when I absolutely knew I wanted to be a teacher. I did that teachery thing where I took control. I batted the little boy off, turned the book around so the kids could see the pictures, and read the rest of the pages upside down.

Small human beings, 40 of them, were totally engrossed. 40 pairs of wide eyes, 40 slack jaws, 40 ramrod straight backs. Not a murmur.

Our point?

Remember your 'best face' – the one Gav asked you to pull half way through the story about the story? That's you at your best.

It's you in 'immersion mode'. It's the wide-eyed, oh-my-gosh-I-can't-wait-for-whatever's-coming-next face. Scientists call it 'flow' – the version of you that is totally absorbed in life, where time passes quickly and everything seems easy.

You did 'that face' a lot when you were 4 and, if you're honest, those wide-eyed moments are tailing off. You still have moments of excitement, where life is unmissable, but the gaps between them are getting longer. Being totally engaged with life – that's worth aiming for. Inching forward towards adventure – that's a wonderful feeling. Enjoying the roller-coaster thrill of life – that's a good way to be.

So after reading our story about a true story about someone telling a story, our actual story begins. Back ramrod straight, legs snapped into place, 'that face' fixed on …

Let's crack on …

Next up, an actual poem.

Part 2
THE INVITATION

It doesn't interest me
what you do for a living.
I want to know
what you ache for
and if you dare to dream
of meeting your heart's longing.

It doesn't interest me
how old you are.
I want to know
if you will risk
looking like a fool
for love
for your dream
for the adventure of being alive.

It doesn't interest me
what planets are
squaring your moon …
I want to know
if you have touched
the centre of your own sorrow
if you have been opened
by life's betrayals
or have become shrivelled and closed
from fear of further pain.

I want to know
if you can sit with pain
mine or your own
without moving to hide it
or fade it
or fix it.
[….]
It doesn't interest me
if the story you are telling me
is true.
I want to know if you can
disappoint another
to be true to yourself.
If you can bear
the accusation of betrayal
and not betray your own soul.
If you can be faithless
and therefore trustworthy.
[….]
I want to know
if you can live with failure
yours and mine
and still stand at the edge of the lake
and shout to the silver of the full moon,
"Yes."

It doesn't interest me
to know where you live
or how much money you have.
I want to know if you can get up
after the night of grief and despair
weary and bruised to the bone
and do what needs to be done
to feed the children.

It doesn't interest me
who you know
or how you came to be here.
I want to know if you will stand
in the centre of the fire
with me
and not shrink back.

It doesn't interest me
where or what or with whom
you have studied.
I want to know
what sustains you
from the inside
when all else falls away.

I want to know
if you can be alone
with yourself
and if you truly like
the company you keep
in the empty moments.

By Oriah 'Mountain Dreamer' House from her book, THE INVITATION © 1999. Published by HarperONE, San Francisco. All rights reserved. Presented with permission of the author. www.oriah.org

Part 3

DEATH (AND HOW TO AVOID IT)

Life: Your Contract

Available for a limited time only.

LIMIT 1 (one) per person.

Subject to change without notice.

Non-transferable and sole responsibility of the user.

NO warranty. **NO** refunds.

Absolutely no guarantee. Of anything!

BREAKAGES have to be <u>PAID</u> for.

Life can have downs as well as ups.

LASTS APPROXIMATELY 4000 WEEKS BUT CONTRACT CAN BE TERMINATED AT ANY TIME AND WITHOUT ANY NOTICE.

Bed of roses, not included. Afterlife, extremely doubtful.

Operating system (your mind) not guaranteed to last as long as your body. Likely to require an update that doesn't yet exist. Until then, oily fish is the only answer.

Terms + Conditions **Apply**. BEST BEFORE: **death**

SIGNATURE: •••••••••••••••••••••••••••••••••••••••

START DATE: •••••••••••••••••••••••••••••••••••••••

EXPECTED EXPIRY DATE:
(start date + 4000 weeks) ••••••••••••••••••••••••

Unleash Your Inner Beyoncé

In 2003, pop music's biggest stars descended upon Edinburgh for the 10th annual MTV Music Awards.

> '…comfort murders the passion of the soul, and then walks grinning at the funeral.'
>
> *Khalil Gibran*

Cue a massive pop-up Big Top which became the centre of the music universe for the night. Leith Council rolled out 200 metres of red carpet for a phalanx of top stars to strut and swagger their way into the Edinburgh lights.

It was a biggie. The paps were a-papping as an estimated one billion people tuned in from across the globe.

And our Gav was there.

Randomly I got an email one day asking if I'd like to get involved with the event as I lived locally and had experience of working in live entertainment. The organizers were looking for people to take on the role of supervisor.

What did this even mean? What needed supervising? Could it be the audience, the staff, or better still, could it be the stars themselves?

Whatever it was, I was in. I was mega keen on working in the entertainment industry and we all have to start somewhere. They were offering a fairly substantial amount of money, I was 23, lived fairly locally and Beyoncé was going to be there. *The* Beyoncé!

I was 100% up to the task. I can supervise superstars. Nothing was going to stop me. This could be the greatest job in the world, and it was being handed to me on a plate.

Along with the other supervisors I was invited to a team meeting. Our instructions were clear …

There were just two rules. Firstly, supervise the shit out of the event because there will be some serious 'names' there. Oh, and wear black. All black. Head to toe black. Shirt, trousers, socks and shoes. Pants too, probably (I might have imagined that bit?).

I had the trousers, shirt, socks and pants but I didn't have black shoes.

So I bought new black shoes. Simple. I was 23, skint and I was only ever going to wear them once so I went for the cheap shoes. They'd be gleaming and new so I'd look the part.

Then came the big night itself. I was tired. I hadn't slept at all the night before. I was excited but I had also bought a new bed recently that just wasn't cutting it. My back was killing me but nothing was going to stop me from breaking into the industry.

Opportunity was knocking. All I had to do was impress all the right people and maybe, just maybe, I could have a dream career in the entertainment business. How could I not be excited?

This was the MTV Music Awards. It was HUGE. And not only was I a part of it, I was *supervising* it. I was going to define a new level of supervision. I was going to be a super-duper-visor. Then I remembered it was a music event so I went higher – I buttoned my black shirt and tied my black shoe laces, winked in the mirror and decided I was going to be a super-trouper-visor. Tonight the lights were gonna find me. I'd be shining like the sun (*sup-p-per troop-p-per*), I'd be smiling having fun (*sup-p-per troop-p-per*) and I was indeed feeling like a number one.

I arrived early to be told where my position for the night would be. Essentially, I was given an area. This included the arena itself and a small backstage area. Remember, my job was to supervise. In other words, to stand for hours and keep an eye out for anything untoward (*fact: I have never typed the word 'untoward' before).

And stand I did. For hours before anyone even started to arrive. My back was slowly getting worse. But I was up for it, I could feel the excitement building around the venue. If my shoulders felt saggy they'd be perked by the occasional quick glimpse of a megastar—an Aguilera, Pink or a Timberlake.

I could hear the noise outside, it was incredible.

Then came the turning point of my night.

As the thousands of excitable teenagers filled the room I began to feel some intense pains in my feet. Now, we've all had blisters before. This was not just your average, everyday blister. For a start, they were plural. I'm talking enormous fuck-off blisters. The ones that are so painful you can't even stand, let alone walk.

Blisters and a bad back.

I wasn't feeling so soo-per-per. I wasn't shining like the sun. This was unbearable. I had a decision to make …

Suck it up, grin and bear it, push through like a champ?

Or …

Be a total wimp, sneak away and get my shoes off asap?

There was one simple question … *what would Beyoncé do?*

Would she allow the blisters to ruin her opportunity? Would she sneak away and get her shoes off? Would she moan and complain to her manager about her sore feet?

WOULD. SHE. FUCK.

She's Beyoncé. She can command over $1,000,000 for a 5-minute performance. She's cool and she goes by one name.

In this moment I stood tall and tried to channel my inner Beyoncé. She'd break out her alter ego, Sacha Fierce, seize the moment and own the whole damn thing.

My alter ego is probably way more Dave the Postman than Sacha Fierce. You see, I'm not anything like Beyoncé. I'm Gavin Oattes from Troon, and I had to get my new shoes off as fast as I could and sit down. My feet were killing me and were clearly about to fall off.

I was about to sit down when the walkie-talkie crackled into life and fresh instructions fed through. I was to move to the smaller backstage area. This meant walking.

WALKING!

I probably had to walk about 100 yards. Each and every step though was torturous. I made a noise as I walked. Phonetically it would be spelled as follows, *'Huuahyaohsshhh'*.

Say it out loud. In fact, say it out loud while limping and you'll get the idea.

I *huuahyaohsshhh*'d my way for 100 yards, wincing and contorted. I got to my next position.

There was no one else around. This was my chance. I could take my shoes off for a while and give my feet a break. Just as I bent down to take them off the door opened and in came a group of people. I quickly stood back up, *'Huuahyaohsshhh'* I said out loud. Everyone turned and looked at me.

The first thing I noticed was how small everyone in the room seemed. Then I realized who they were. In the exact same space as me were the following …

Kylie Minogue, Christina Aguilera and Justin Hawkins, lead singer of The Darkness. Pop and rock royalty.

And then it happened.

The door opened and in came Beyoncé. The most famous and powerful woman on the planet. Sacha Fierce herself.

And all I could think about was my red hot soles. By this stage the pain had reached a whole new level. My feet were channelling their own Sacha Fierce.

This was my moment to say hello to these people, to become their new best friend, to launch my brand new career in celeb-land.

Do NOT mess this one up Gav I thought to myself. *Just turn, smile and say hello.* I turned, I smiled and a blister burst. My feet were on fire. I needed to take my shoes off. I couldn't. Not in front of Beyoncé, Kylie, Christina and Justin.

Just at this stage I was radioed once again to change positions. I was to head back out to the arena. I *huuahyaohsshhh-ed* back to my original position – this time sobbing in pain – and never saw Beyoncé again.

The night came to an end and I left.

I got on the night bus to head home. To finally sit down felt like a dream.

The bus broke down and I had to walk the last 3 miles. I chucked my shoes and walked in my bare feet, the cold pavement felt amazing on my burning soles.

It's only now that I can look back and contemplate my experience.

Honestly? Crap. The music was crap, the venue was crap, the job was crap, my new shoes were crap and my new bed was crap.

But what did I learn?

No matter who you are or where life is taking you, always buy decent shoes and a decent bed. If you're not in one, then you're in the other. It matters.

I also learned I'm not Beyoncé and that I don't belong in her world.

And that's okay.

Because *Zest* isn't about celeb culture. Neither is it about pretending to be someone you're not.

It's about squeezing every last drop out of who you already are.

An Inside Job

> ### Beschaulich. German:
> Quiet, pensive; living a simple life; pleasantly contemplative, unhurried in a fashion that inspires mental well-being.

Foraging around in the academic undergrowth, you do occasionally find some well-hidden gems that (for reasons that will become obvious) resonate deeply with me. Quirky stuff. I bloomin' love it!

Your name, for starters. A middle initial makes people think you're smarter. It's a general rule that has one or two notable exceptions (e.g. George W. Bush). Also, if your initials are closer to 'A', the better your chances of getting into a top university. As 'Andy Cope' I'm liking that study. I'm imagining Zinedine Zidane never went to school at all?

Good news. Your author tag team all went to school. We've all had hard knocks so be reassured, we're coming at life from a real-world perspective.

Unbridled go-getting isn't our thing. An enthusiastic *'Woohoo, another restructure at work. That means there'll be fewer of us so more space to spread out,'* is likely to get you a punch on the nose.

We prefer a brand of realistic optimism. Reining Pollyanna in just a tad gets you to a point of seeing the possibilities and maybe asking yourself *what's the best that could happen?*

Does that require rose-tinted specs? We think there's definitely some mileage in learning to see life through an optimistic hue but trust us, you don't need new glasses. We're not offering a new prescription, just a good clean. Because here's the thing: if you scrape the shit off the lenses you're currently wearing everything looks a whole lot clearer.

Jimmy Cliff might not have made the same impact on the charts with 'I can see clearly now the shit has gone' but he would have seen all obstacles in his way and, indeed, he might have had a bright (bright) sunshiny day.

Seeing clearly. Sounds simple enough? So hands up if you actually read the poetry in Part 2?

We reckon that about 50% of readers won't have bothered to see it clearly. Why? Because it's long, a bit heavy – not many laughs – and you think poems should rhyme, right?

In which case you'll have done what the old me would have done and rolled your eyes at an overly long, heavyweight, non-rhyming poem.

If you skipped it, please go back a few pages and do something you wouldn't normally do.

Read it *slooooowly.* Read it twice.

Because gosh, it's powerful from the first word to the last. But it's this particular bit that we would like to focus on:

> *It doesn't interest me*
> *where or what or with whom*
> *you have studied.*
> *I want to know*
> *what sustains you*
> *from the inside*
> *when all else falls away.*

That's our exact starting point for *Zest*.

It makes no odds what you already know. No matter how many PhDs you've got, life is going to challenge you. Life can be awesome, but it can also be cruel, relentless and unforgiving. There will be times when it feels like it's trying to break you.

So when those times come it makes sense to be ready, and that's very much an inside job.

Hard Knocks

I'll never forget my grandad's last words to me … 'What bus?'

Supposedly, death and taxes are the only two certainties in life. Then you find out that multi-gazillion dollar Amazon pays almost no tax – so it's just death then.

Hey ho! Life's not fair. We acknowledge that there are different rules for the super-rich. The rest of us crack on with life on the understanding that none of us will get out alive.

My great-grandad used to say, 'Knock hard lad, because life's deaf', and I never really understood what he meant until I was older.

And he was long gone.

It's worth contrasting his world with my children's world. Let's nip back three generations to your *great* grandparents' days …

Leaving aside the miracle of surviving two world wars, life was physically exhausting. Those gathering the harvest, choking down the pit or toiling in the factory would get home full of aches and pains. They'd eat and sleep and toil again. You don't have to go back far to understand that men were employed because of their physical prowess. Death often came well before retirement.

And women? Three generations ago, by and large, they weren't employed. Your *great-great*-grandma didn't have time, what with all the raising of your great-grandma and her six siblings.

There were clear roles and societal structures. With no central heating and very little indoor plumbing, life was tough. Imagine, they didn't even have coffee. Or electricity. Or supermarkets. Or pizzas.

Look around at the world today. Gosh! Modernity. We have no desire to do away with our comfy central-heated ensuite bathroom'd fully carpeted homes, or to hark back to the 'good old days' of rickets and diphtheria. The modern world is uber-comfy with a Starbucks on every street and deep pan pepperoni deliver-ood to your door. Our *great-great*-grandparents would be amazed at what we have! We're the first generation in the history of human beings to have more than we need.

Amongst an abundance of abundance the question is, *are we any happier?*

Because the big 'BUT' is this: back in the day, the miners lived in the pit village. They didn't have to commute. Work was 8 to 5 and then you clocked off. The workers didn't go home and log onto their emails. The hashtag hadn't been invented. They didn't have to spend 25% of their day remembering passwords. Their teenage daughters didn't have to measure up to airbrushed perfection. Their boys didn't feel the urge to take pictures of their private parts and share them via smartphones.

The pit village has been replaced by a commuter town, just 90 minutes each way on the train. So your *great-great*-grandparents 8 a.m. to 5 p.m. has morphed into your 6 a.m. to 8 p.m. The coalface has been replaced by the typeface. After a hard day at the office you slump into your you-shaped sofa sarcophagus and log back on to work.

A lot of the physical labour has gone. Instead, danger lurks, stealth-like, in the pace of life. It's not obvious to the eye. The physicality has been replaced by sheer full-on-ness that can grind you down. We feel emotionally and mentally depleted. Whereas those doing physical jobs suffered from bad backs, cricked necks, vibration white finger, crushed limbs and emphysema, the new millennium has seen the rise of anxiety, stress, panic attacks, loneliness, suicide, self-harm and full-blown depression.

My sex life is like a Ferrari.

I don't have a Ferrari.

And that's our starting point. We don't want to 'go back' to a different time. Those times have gone. But we'd like to help you 'get back' to being you at your best. If the world has changed, then so must we. Plugging back into the full-wattage high-energy version of yourself is the key to your mental wealth.

It also happens to be your gift to the world. Human beings are wired to catch each other's emotions, so when you shine brightly, it also lights up your nearest and dearest.

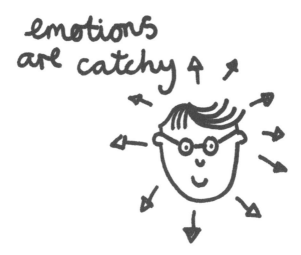

The big BUT becomes a huge HOW?

How are we supposed to shine when the modern world seems hell-bent on dimming and dulling us?

That huge question brings us to a massive answer. In a sentence that many gurus have hinted at but never dared say, here's the answer. Gav's answer:

If there's no light at the end of the tunnel then light the fucker up yourself.

I'm pretty sure that's what my great-grandad was trying to say.

A Series of Fortunate Events

You started off as stardust and you'll finish-up as worm-fodder. In the evolutionary heartbeat between, an improbable flicker of luminescent humanity, you exist. But you owe it to yourself to exist *fully*, both in mind and body.

In sanity, not insanity.

There's a wonderfully cheesy meme about the past being history, the future a mystery, today is a gift, which is why we call it 'the present'.

In which case we'd like to add extra cheese. If life is, indeed, a short and precious gift let's not send it back unwrapped.

Death, I imagine, is going to be a real bummer. Not just the lifelessness and zero breathing malarkey, but the inevitability of the damn thing. The sobering thought isn't death per se, it's the fact that I'm going to spend a very long time being dead.

We spend an average of 29,000 days being alive. That's just over 4000 weeks in old money. It's quite focusing to realize that when you get to the ripe old age of 40 you're closer to the end than the beginning.

Of course, if you lived forever – if you had infinity to mess around in – nothing would matter. But if you've only got 4000 weeks then EVERYTHING MATTERS!

I'm going to spend the whole of infinity *minus* 4000 weeks, being dead. And infinity's a helluva big number. I know because when I was eight me and my mate tried counting it.

Working the logic the other way, being alive – your 4000 weeks – that should be totes amazing. All that zesty freshness. Smacking up all that yummy oxygen.

But there's an uncomfortable paradox sitting at the heart of it all. 4000 weeks isn't a huge amount of time but it's a long time to be going through the motions.

> **Fact:** Pessimists don't live longer than optimists. It just feels like it!

Rather than carping about death being too long and life being too short, we're more interested in making sure that your alive part is properly alive. The bigger question might therefore be *are you living your 29,000 days, or are you living the same day 29,000 times?*

We've all experienced déjà vu but, more recently I've started experiencing the modern-day equivalent, déjà *moo*: when you're sitting in a meeting and you're overwhelmed by a feeling that you've heard all this bullshit before.

In a book that sets out to celebrate human flourishing, it's important to acknowledge the facts. Look around on your morning commute and, despite the brevity of life, you'll not see much zestiness.

There's a lot of déjà moo-ing.

Very few folk dance around the kitchen in their pyjamas. I'm struggling to recall the last time I witnessed someone skipping to work. It's a sad indictment of modern-day life that work isn't working. Many of us don't enjoy it, feel undervalued and bemoan our lot betwixt Monday and Friday. The weekends provide an opportunity to get even more worked-up, as the prospect of the next dollop of drudgery looms ever closer. We're either doing or ruing; suffering or worrying. We're alive but not truly living.

Fact: Being morose and seemingly devoid of humour doesn't make you appear more professional in any way, just morose and devoid of humour.

What we're not about to do is tell you to embrace your role as a low-paid, perpetually put-upon bullshit-shifter. Neither are we going to tell you that it's all in your head. It's not. If you need to be dragged to work kicking and screaming every Monday, we get it. But just because it IS like that doesn't mean it has to STAY like it. Personal change is for the sake of you *and everyone around you*. The italics is important. A better version of you creates an emotional uplift for your nearest and dearest. If you can't be arsed to eat healthy, get fit, change jobs or quit grumbling – do it for them!

There is always something that can be done to change for the better. Or there is always something that can be done to *start* the change to a change for the better.

Zest is the start.

Too many people are experiencing a near-life experience. That's *their* norm. But don't be fooled by the sleight-of-hand dealt by expectations. Your 'normal' can be different to theirs.

Your 'normal' doesn't mean you have to replicate the rituals and routines of the indoctrinated masses; 'following', 'liking' and courting acceptance from invisible multitudes. 'Normal', doesn't mean fitting in, blindly accepting and agreeing, eternally commuting without ever arriving.

'Normal' means to feel completely and utterly 'you'. To feel calm and comforted in your own skin; existing within personal parameters that allow you to flow. 'Normal', is unique; different; a genetic once-in-any-lifetime combination that only fits one glass slipper.

So why bother tortuously forcing yourself to fit in when you can re-set 'normal' to 'epic', 'extraordinary' or 'stand-out amazing'?

We dare to ask the BIG questions …
What is true about you today that would make your eight-year-old self cry?

Think back to when you were three. Chances are, there was always someone who was likely carried in to school sobbing hysterically that needed to be peeled away from a grown-up's knee. It may even have been you. Parents subsequently scuttle out of the classroom, heads down, off to embark upon their day, feeling decidedly inadequate, upset and mildly traumatized by the whole experience. Of course, what they don't see, is that by the time they've exited the school gates, Little Miss/Mr Hysteria is happily immersed in a game of Lego, practically the life and soul of Club 3 to 4.

Our point? We can become entrenched in a certain way of thinking where everything is pants. When you were knee-high, you could be down one minute but happily skipping about the next. Being down doesn't have to mean you have to stay down, and certainly doesn't mean you're 'out'.

You're very much 'in': *in*volved, *in* control of your feelings and *in* charge of how you react and respond to the world. The trick is to accept there's going to be downs, but recognize that you don't have to stay there.

It's okay to snap out of it, and it's okay to buck-up. It's okay to deviate. You don't have to have a period of mourning on a Monday morning.

The Fanciful French

Vivre sans temps mort. (Live without wasted time.)

Parisian political slogan

We witness 'imposter syndrome' to the power of a hundred. Normal imposter syndrome is the feeling of being found out. We're talking about the fear of finding out you're an imposter of who you once were. A doppelganger of yourself. You look in the mirror and it sure looks like you, but deep down you know it's a pale imitation of the person you *could* be.

You *used* to be.

You *want* to be again.

It doesn't have to be like this. Everything that you once felt, and the promise that existed, is still there. 'That time' is still now. But to find it, you must first find – or *rediscover* – the real you.

Scratching around for a book title we chanced upon 'ZEST'. Nice word. We looked it up. The dictionary definition includes great words like zingy, enthusiasm, energy, gusto, eagerness, zeal and fervour. Or, even better, zest equates to passion, love, enjoyment, excitement and delight.

It also connotes a tang, a sharpness. Plunge your teeth into a freshly sliced lemon and there's a certain kick!

It's the opposite of bland.

Zest is also an outer layer and it's this that swung the title. We want to get under your skin. Not in a 'burrowing worm that lays eggs' way, but in a 'challenging your thinking' way. When you zest an orange you remove all the pith. We'll be doing a lot of that – taking the pith – because ultimately, we want this to be a rollicking good read.

These pages will challenge you to dream big, work hard, learn well, celebrate your failures and love unconditionally.

We want to help you be your zesty best on a more regular basis.

Googling, Goggling and Ogling

You won't know what a subphylum Urochordata is, until we give you its more common name, the sea squirt.

Then you begin to picture it. You've seen hundreds of them, clamped to rocks and piers. 'Sea squirt' describes its existence, letting sea water in at one end – filtering the nutrients – and squirting it out the other end.

It's not unhappy with its deal. *Water in … filter … and expel.* The thing about the sea squirt is that it doesn't know there's more to life. It doesn't ponder. It doesn't reminisce. It doesn't dream of better days ahead. It's a hermaphrodite, which means it doesn't need a mate. The fact that it can make love to itself is quite handy because it doesn't have to make an effort to look super sexy and gorgeous.

Handy, that!

Water in … out … with a little shaking it all about.

Why doesn't the sea squirt raise its aspirations? The simple answer is because it can't. Because when it was a baby squirt it paddled around until it found a rock, attached itself, got comfy and then ate its own brain. The squirt brain is useful in finding something to attach to but, once that bit's done, it doesn't need to think anymore so it scoffs it, thus providing a bit of sustenance so it can hang on for the rest of its dear life.

Sea Squirt

AKA: Brainless!

Might there be a human equivalent? People who have settled on their rock and, metaphorically, eaten their brains.

Maybe it's time for a rethink? A rethinking of *how* we think!

Let's take the modern phenomenon of busyness. We're all super busy. But we may well be busy doing the wrong things. If, as surveys suggest, young people are spending nine hours a day online (which incidentally is more time than they spend sleeping) then by age 80 they will have clocked up 30 solid years of Wi-Fi access.

That's a lot of screen time.

So it's worth considering what we are doing with that screen time?

The empty text box, that's what.

'What's on your mind?' Facebook asks. Twitter beckons with 'Compose a new tweet.' The comments section at the bottom of the article you just read. Blank spaces, begging to be filled in with thoughts, with photos, with stories.

Often with nothing. At least, nothing *important*.

Technology, asking you, prodding you, soliciting talk.

We're a species that's googling, ogling and goggling. Googling ourselves, checking we're included in the Internet of things. Ogling at porn. Seduced by cat videos. Clodhopping through a load of clickbait to ogle at what your favourite 80s TV star looks like now.

In Britain there's a TV series called *Gogglebox* which I'm led to believe is where we, the intelligent viewers, get to watch people watching television. One day soon I'm going to record myself watching *Gogglebox* and post it on FaceTube so people can watch me watching people watching people watch TV. Then maybe you can record yourself watching my FaceTube channel and we can keep adding people until the world's watching people watching people watching people watching people watching people watch TV … until the penny finally drops in a mass *kerching* moment of realization.

Virtually living isn't actually living. I've eaten my fucking brain! I've been sucked into a vortex of meaninglessness. *Why am I seduced into doing this shit?*

Here's a controversial thought …

What if our frantic days are really just a magician's sleight of hand that draws your attention away from the real problem.

Which is?

Emptiness.

Maybe you hide it well, smiling limply whilst haemorrhaging conviction and purpose. Listen carefully. The silence is screaming; a deafening tinnitus continuously pounding the insides of your mind, threatening to shatter any last remaining vestiges of sanity.

What if our 'busyness' serves as a kind of inner reassurance – obviously your life cannot possibly be empty, trivial or meaningless if you are so ridiculously busy, completely booked up and in demand every hour of the day?

Back-to-back meetings; *gosh I must be important.*

Working into the evenings; *jeez, I've got a lot of important deadlines.*

Hours on social media; *crikey, I've got a lot of online chums. They'll need to know what I've had for tea.*

What if we've become superb at masquerading as 'busy' to paper over the nagging feeling that 'something's missing'. I think this is, at the very least, an interesting thought and, at very best, an earth-shattering realization.

But how can something be missing when we literally have everything?

A smorgasbord of freedom and choice is laid out before us. Everything's available, in material abundance. We're the first generation in the history of human beings to be dying from excess.

Fact: there are 361 different types of yoghurt at my local supermarket. Hand on heart, I have counted them. I actually went with pen and pad – not a shopping list – I was *making* a list, counting the items on the shelves. Calculating choices, so I could report back. There are 994 ways to buy chocolate and 1556 types of alcohol to quench my thirst for happiness. There's a choice of 581 ready meals for those who lack time and skill to cook. There is pre-grated cheese, pre-mashed potato, frozen omelette, pre-packaged salad, peeled oranges and ready peeled hard-boiled eggs.

The materialistic world has bent over backwards to give you everything you ever wanted, and much more besides.

'…thousands of people are out there leading lives of quiet, screaming desperation, where they work long, hard hours at jobs they hate to enable them to buy things they don't need to impress people they don't like.'

Nigel Marsh

41

Here's the thing. When life's laid out in an amazing technicolour of abundance, what's a person supposed to do other than gorge?

Materialism is so moreish and consumption its most obvious strategy. Look around at those chasing more – fat people eating more pizza, teenagers downloading more data, lonely people hooked on their laptop, alcoholics supping more Tennent's Extra, workaholics toiling longer – and ask yourself, *is it working?*

Is the best strategy merely to avail yourself of everything simply because you can? It's the same as snogging your sister – just because you can doesn't always mean you should.

The emptiness, it's not lack of stuff.

Amid the Googling, goggling and ogling, eventually it dawns that the missing piece in your life is most probably you. Yes, you are lacking you!

Being happy with who you are. Being happy with your lot. It's called contentment and it's a kind of magic.

Because this is how it works. We're not suggesting that buying stuff is a bad thing to do. If you plot income and happiness on a chart, at no point does 'having more money' make you less happy. Buying stuff doesn't make you unhappy. But the *relentless pursuit of more* – that will make you unhappy.

Knowing when to stop is crucial. Learning to be content with what you already have means you can quit the chase.

Quitting the chase – THAT will make you happy.

A Toast, to Some Toast

As Will pens this, his wife has just returned from a foray to the local charity shop. It wasn't a random, impulsive expedition – more of a return visit. A calling that could no longer be ignored.

Her booty? A full dinner set: plates – six small, medium and large, with matching dishes. Quite a haul. I admit to having a special liking for plates, largely because they hold lasagne, stew or toast. But even to my untrained eye, these are special. Beautiful. Each piece is ornately decorated china, consisting of light blue etchings and illustrations circumnavigated with silver-gilded edging.

They are works of art probably dating back to the 1950s. Despite their advancing years, they are in pristine condition, belying their fragile intricacies and still looking their best.

Their Sunday Best.

Judging by appearances, it seems this beloved 24-piece dinner set has rarely been dined upon.

Someone's pride and joy has languished in a glass display cabinet, waiting … waiting for such a time worthy of justifiable celebration and utilization. That time, in all probability, came infrequently.

If ever.

Their owner was waiting and waiting [and waiting and waiting] for the perfect opportunity to use their best china.

They died waiting.

And now, they've been purchased in a branch of the British Red Cross for the princely sum of ten pounds. Ten pounds; the price sticky-labelled upon someone's lifelong pride and joy, the price deemed representative of someone's most special of occasions. The 'best', that only manifested in a month of Sundays, if at all.

Now I'd like to assure you, reader, that they've gone to a good home. Each and every plate will be used, rotated and incorporated into daily life, accommodating a vast array of misfits (including teenagers), in celebration, commiseration and sometimes just to eat.

They are my go-to plates. They will be present on the best and worst of Mondays to Fridays, in addition to weekends. But part of me wished I'd inherited them in slightly worse condition – perhaps with the odd chip – or maybe with one of the saucers missing, even.

Because how often do we put off our best in subconscious preference for enduring below-par? We keep our potential in reserve, rather than actually exploring it, revelling in it – just in case it's not as precious as we'd like to think. We hide rather than shine. We gather dust until we turn to dust.

Our pristine charity shop purchase serves as a warning. Don't resign yourself to a ten-pound charity-shop epitaph; live and ensure you leave your mark on the world like only you can.

Act Your Shoe Size

'Walking across the playground.'

'I don't know where I'm going from here, but I promise it won't be boring.'

David Bowie

There's so much wrong about that sentence (ignoring the fact it's not actually a sentence).

If we were to insert the word 'children' at the beginning, it might make it grammatically correct, but at the same time even more wrong. Offensive even. It's a toxic oxymoron – a toxymoron; a contradiction in terms; an affront to every self-respecting seven-year-old currently revelling in their daily 15 minutes of sheer unadulterated joy. And if it doesn't bother you, then it should.

Playgrounds, you see, are meant to be played on. They're the battlegrounds of orcs and sorcerers, transformers and stegosauruses. They're Strictly dance floors and Pineapple Studios, dramatic backdrops and sought-after centre circles. Walking just doesn't cut it.

Think back. The playground was a backdrop to discovery, adventure, first times, full-times and finding. You've huddled in sub-zero temperatures refusing point-blank to wear a coat because … because no one else does. You've spilt crisps on that playground. Monster Munch. Maybe Space Invaders. If you're under 30, you've eaten cheese strings on that playground.

Cheese? *In a string?* You weirdo.

A PLAY-ground. The clue's in the name. It's to be played on.

And now?

The brass handbell has well and truly rung. Not for everyone, but for most, playtime has ended. The memories can seem very distant; so removed from the person you are now, the adult that you accidentally became. We reach for the remote, no longer for the stars. We shrug. We don't rise and shine, instead we rise and whine.

You've become an adult but you don't have to be adulterated. Playtime doesn't have to be finished. You're still here. You're the very same you from bygone days. You've never really been away, you just need to find the way again. We're throwing you a lifeline, a rectangular, paper-backed Zesty buoyancy aid. You just need to remember.

You're not old, just older. You're not grown-up, just growing. You're not stuck when you can twist.

> 'Everyone is different, which means that anyone can fit in.'
>
> *Paddington Bear*

Looking around at the grown-ups in your life you'll notice that, by and large, they've forgotten how to play. We've come to expect and accept the expected, bridling at the thought of spontaneity. So it's time to reclaim your inner Action Man, your secret Sindy, and put the Evil back into your Knievel.

Pimp your life so that it's no longer just another off-the-rail replica. That doesn't mean you've got to trail around the metropolis with your favourite toy. It doesn't mean you have to dangle it from any windows with your dressing-gown belt.

[Although you could, if you fancied it?]

What it does mean, is that you've got to put yourself out there.

Somewhere along the line we exchange our shoe age for our chronological age, and I'm not entirely sure it's at all a good thing.

This leads us to a barrage of massive WHAT IFs?

What if we treated life a little bit more like playtime? If we treated it as a blank tarmac canvas, ripe for projecting our dreams and aspirations.

What if your lifetime was in fact one long playtime?

What if the meaning of life was, well, to be lively?

What if our purpose was to enjoy rather than to endure, to relish rather than resent, to engage rather than enrage? What if the best way to avoid death was to stay young?

Shoesize? I'm 8½. Yep, that sounds about right.

The Sunlounger Principle

So to finish our death chapter, we'll leave you with a little something from Gav. It's a case study in aliveness. For the moments you think you've not got any zing, think again. When your passion's been extinguished, think 'Sunlounger Principle'.

Gav, take it away …

So what is 'The Sunlounger Principle'? In its simplest form SLP (like NLP, but fewer big words) is a technique that enables you to quickly get to grips with a task you perhaps otherwise can't be fucked doing. It creates an instant whoosh of botheredness, whether that be pinging out of bed on a Monday morning, tidying the house, cooking, going to the gym or even studying.

Not only does our SLP technique guarantee that you will do said task but that you'll do it with energy, enthusiasm, vigour and a great big 'I'M A FUCKING NINJA AT THIS' attitude.

We can feel your scepticism. Calm that inner voice. This is the principle: *You treat every single day as if it was one big fat marvellous summer vacation.*

Hang in there. Let us soothe your scepticism with some facts.

Think about a time you spent an absolute fortune to get away for two weeks chill-out in the sun. You'd been dreaming about it for 12 months. You could almost taste it the closer it got. Sunshine, me time, family time, beautiful food and drink, pure magic. Bliss.

You arrive.

You dump your bags in your room and decide to have a nosey around, you know, get your bearings.

You're scoping the joint.

But for what?

A prime sunlounger spot. That's fucking what. Some folk have to work at it but for others SLP comes naturally. It's practically subconscious. Stealth-like.

Like all ninja-related activity, there are details. And levels. I mean there's stuff to think about. Space, shade, direction, chavs, bar, pool, noise, water polo, the other chavs and how far you are from your room.

Joint thoroughly cased, you enjoy your first balmy evening out, fizzy lagers are supped, bag packed, the alarm is set very early and you fall into a fitful sleep. You're coiled, and then *BEEEEEP*, the alarm sounds.

It's like the gun going off at the Olympics. On the B of
BEEEEEEP, you're out of bed, heart pounding, adrenaline
rushing. You struggle into a tee-shirt and stagger around your
hotel room as you put both feet though one pant hole. Your
self-belief is through the roof, you grab your pre-packed bag
and take 10 seconds to survey the scene. Your sleeping wife
reminds you why you're up so early. *I'm doing it for her.* You
take a peek at your children, asleep in the twin room. *I'm
doing this for love.*

And you're gone. You press the lift button as a decoy but there's
no waiting. You're leaping three stairs at a time, barefooted,
down and down, slamming the lift button on every floor.

You arrive at your destination. A few SLPers have the same idea
and you're frustrated but you can't help admire them. Seasoned
pros.

There's a gap, and you're in. It's a bit of effort pulling four lone
sunbeds from different parts of the pool and there's a terrible
scraping sound as you drag the one with dodgy wheels. But,
mission accomplished. Okay, they're not matching ones, plus
one has a faulty back and another a stuck wheel, but you've
assembled a quartet and for that, your family will be grateful.

You furtively unzip your pre-packed backpack, you pull four beach
towels and lay them, one per bed.

Wonderful.

It's only now that you can relax. You puff your cheeks out in
exhausted pride. Time to evaluate. *Success, but I cut it fine. These*

were the last four beds. And you know your patch will shade over after 2 p.m. *Tomorrow, I will have to be earlier, particularly if I want that patch over there, where the sun lingers all day.* You've noticed that's where the leathery brown elderly Germans set out their camp. They're the benchmark. You want to be them, but not German and without the thongs.

A harried-looking man enters the arena, hair askew, eyes still half shut. He'd been waiting for the lift. He looks around and curses. *Amateur. Snoozing is losing*, you think. *An SLP novice. How's he going to explain this to his family?*

Job done, you retire upstairs, this time via the lift. Lifts are good for thinking. What is it about sunloungers? They bring out a side in people that if channelled could be put to some real good in life. The passion. The energy. The hunger. The early start. Not to mention planning, creativity, commitment, purpose and effort. Take it and apply it to shit in your life that matters.

Your health. Your family. Your career. *Get fucking bothered!*

The sun is peeping over the horizon. It's bedtime. It's 5.55 a.m. and you've seized the day.

You own the fucking day.

Carpe-fucking-diem, indeed.

Part 4
KOOL RULES 4 LIFE

> '…the only people for me are the mad ones, the ones who are mad to live, mad to talk, mad to be saved, desirous of everything at the same time, the ones who never yawn or say a commonplace thing, but burn, burn, burn like fabulous yellow roman candles exploding like spiders across the stars…'
>
> Jack Kerouac, On the Road

The 1970s popster Kool (and not forgetting his gang) was mad keen that we ce-le-brate good times. *Come on!*

In homage to his misspelt name (his actual name was Bob, thanks Wiki) we're devoting this chapter to what we're calling our 'Kool Rules 4 Life'. If Bob's right, and there really is a party going on, right here, these rules will help bring good times and laughter too, cos we're gonna celebrate your party with you.

Think of this humble offering as the basics. Moses had some commandments etched on a tablet (an old style tablet, that is) but his were different. His Top 10 were how to live your life. Not tapping off with next door's wife, avoid killing people, stealing is bad – these are inarguably great rules for maintaining the neighbourhood peace and staying out of prison.

We're not saying we've outdone Moses. That'd be stupid, right? If we out-commanded his commandments he'd be sure to send boils, frogs or locusts and we don't want to risk any of that nonsense.

So we've updated the list. Ours isn't a list to abide by. It's not a list of things you need to do, it's 10 things that, in today's world, just are.

Our plan is to drop them in and then revisit them later.

All of them.

Onwards …

Kool Rule 1 – You will receive a body

Look in the mirror. Have a prod around at your chest, tap your skull, wrinkle your nose, stamp your feet, pat your tummy. Flick a nipple. *Ouch!* Yes, that's a body, for sure.

Whether you love it or hate it, your body is your means of getting around town and it's like a new-style supermarket shopping bag; it's for life. So accept it. It's the only one you'll ever have. Let's tell you something you already know; there will be lumps and bumps and sticky out bits. And maybe a mole where you don't want one. And that mole might have its own individual hair? You'll have some or all of wonky teeth, big ears, muffin tops, a wrinkle (or two), grey hair, no hair, flat feet, big boobs, little boobs, big moobs, love handles, etc.

There's definitely going to be something that wobbles.

You'll be drawn to your imperfections. The key is to acknowledge and love them.

You didn't ask for this particular body. You were given it. It's a gift. Treat it as such. There's no receipt so you can't return it so make the most of it and always remember what really counts is what's inside. This sounds like a bit of a cliché, but it's true. Eat good food (most of the time) and sleep well (always). Take your body for a brisk walk every single day.

'You are not your job, you're not how much money you have in the bank. You are not the car you drive. You're not the contents of your wallet. You are not your fucking khakis.'

Chuck Palahniuk, Fight Club

The other thing about your body is that it's not actually you. It's the mode of transport you use to get the *real you* around town. That's the bit that needs unpicking! Look in the mirror and, I agree, it sure looks like you.

If you wave, it waves back.

The *real* you is the one inside your head. The YOU we're interested in is the one who's aware that you're a bunch of molecules that's become aware that it's a bunch of molecules. The awareness of self. The YOU that contemplates, reminisces, dreams, intuits and rationalizes. Yes, all the stuff that your average sea squirt cannot do.

'The first principle is that you must not fool yourself – and you are the easiest person to fool.'

Richard Feynman

This book is for the YOU who can stand in front of a mirror, look at your reflection and wonder who's the one that's aware that you're looking at you? Who's the one aware that you're waving?

If we can engage that person, your lovely wobbly imperfections will follow.

Kool Rule 2 – You will be presented with lessons

For the self-help aficionados you'll recognize this as classic NLP territory (there are no mistakes, *blah blah*). For those who haven't heard of NLP, well done you.

'You will be presented with lessons' is, on balance, a good thing, but only if you learn them! It's easy to NOT learn them. Equally perplexing, it's a doddle to learn the wrong ones!

You are programmed to learn. In fact, you're a learning machine, which is actually rather awesome because, let's face it, life is a constant learning experience … soak it up.

Get addicted.

Become a learning junkie.

Kool Rule 3 – Haters gonna hate

This third rule brings us back down with a bit of a bump. Those haters! Taylor Swift, who knew she'd turn out to be so right?

'If you really hate someone tell them NOW in case they die unexpectedly. Bad-mouthing them when they're dead is still fun, though.'

One of the wickedly satirical #ArdaghTips

We call ourselves 'human*kind*', but sometimes our kindness halos can slip. The milk of human kindness can feel, at best, a bit semi-skimmed.

Kindness is a superpower. It's up there with 'niceness' as the ultimate human character trait. Two points worth noting. First, kindness doesn't have to cost anything. A smile, a chat, an open door, make someone a cuppa, tell someone they're ace, give a hug, hold a hand, let someone into the traffic, pay a compliment.

Second, being kind by nature is great but surprising yourself with your spontaneity is even better. *Random* acts of kindness are sublime because everyone wins. *Anonymous* random acts of kindness are ninja level. Day made and nobody knows it was you. The anonymity somehow makes your day.

But no matter how fabulous you are, there will always be detractors. The modern world has made it easier than ever to be a hater. In the olden days (BC: Before Computers) haters might have whispered behind your back or had a grumble in their head, but now they can tap away at a keyboard and spit bile at anyone and everyone. That's why *virtual* courage is yellow. It's amazing how brave a keyboard can make you.

So rule #3 has a tag line. Sure, haters are gonna hate in the same way that it's hurt people who hurt people. Our tagline is this: *If you can't beat 'em, definitely don't join 'em.*

'When they *go* low, we *go* high.'
Michelle Obama

Be an encourager not a hater.

Our challenge to you is this: be a kindness ninja. That means being super-kind to everyone. Yes, even the one or two idiots who don't seem to deserve it. If they're not very nice people that's because they've not experienced enough kindness or love.

So love the unloved, be nice to the not-so-nice and be kind to the unkind.

Amen.

Kool Rule 4 – Plot twists are coming whether you want them or not

Let me guess, shit always happens to you, right?

The dirty little truth is that shit happens to everyone. Sure, some people seem to have more of it to contend with but bad stuff is a consequence of being alive. Life isn't fair and the other dirty little truth is that *nobody ever said it was*. Try starting from the position that life isn't ever going to be fair and you'll feel your angst washing away.

Once you've twigged that work is supposed to be challenging, parenting is tough and it rains a lot in British seaside towns, the unfairness begins to lose its grip. Of course, we're talking about not sweating the small stuff of which, we promise, most of it is. How many times do you shout at the news or roll your eyes or get home from work and grumble, 'Holy crap, guess what happened to me today?'

Because that's what conventional wisdom tells us to do. In a bizarre daily ritual, we've learned to offload all the detritus on the people we love the most. Brace yourself for an uncomfortable sentence. Coming through the door and offloading your shit merely pebble-dashes your family with emotional diarrhoea.

Our *unconventional* wisdom dares to challenge the validity of time-honoured tradition. Yes, it might actually be true that your day has been a total disaster. Your train was late, your meetings went horribly, an angry customer yelled at you and another round of redundancies was announced. But here's the killer question: *was it a bad day or was it a bad 5 minutes that you've been milking all day?*

In a previous book, Gav argued that your daily challenges are not a 'nightmare' and that your train being delayed for three minutes does not constitute your 'worst day ever'. It's self-inflicted #FakeStress.[1] Think of your daily challenges as plot twists. In fact we encourage you to shout them out! So when the tannoy announces that your train is delayed and everyone else rolls their eyes and chunters under their breath, feel free to yell out 'plot twist!'.

Elvis (the English version who didn't eat peanut butter, banana and bacon sarnies and who is therefore still alive) sang that 'every day you write the book' and he's bang on the money. Every day is a page of the story of your life. All the best books have a plot twist – the really good ones keep you guessing with several – the things you didn't see coming, the pages that take your breath away.

It's helpful to examine the same point but in reverse. Imagine a story with no plot twists? It'd be a plodding, predictable, stale affair. With everything second guessed, there'd be no point reading it. Like a roller coaster that just goes all smooth and flat. A roller coaster with no twists and turns is just a … *coaster.*

Guaranteed there's no queue for that particular ride.

Enjoy your plot twists. They make the ride worthwhile.

----

[1] *Check out www.weworry4u.co.uk for a glorious send-up of Fake Stress.*

59

Kool Rule 5 – Life is a sausage machine

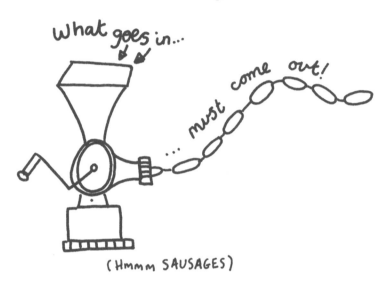

What goes in... ...must come out!

(Hmmm SAUSAGES)

What you make of your life is up to you.

Where you are right now is a direct result of decisions that you have made. That doesn't always seem very fair (remember 'plot twists' in rule #4?) but it's true.

You have all the tools and resources you need. You are bursting with potential. No pressure, but what you do with it is up to you.

Richard Wilkins, self-styled 'Minister of Inspiration', likens life to a sausage machine. Use your vivid imagination to imagine such a contraption. You know the routine – the ingredients go in at one end, you turn a handle and an endless string of sausages is squeezed out of the other end. If you wanted pork sausages you'd stick a squealing piggy in at the ingredients end. If you wanted vegan sausages, you'd put squealing vegans in. Without insulting your intelligence, if you wanted Quorn sausages, you wouldn't stick a horse in. It just doesn't work like that.

And then there's life itself. Imagine the same sausage machine principle, but instead of sausages, it's now your life, the precious 4000 weeks that you've been granted. Same routine, so you stuff the ingredients of life in at one end, turn the handle and your life is squeezed out of the other end. Keep turning the handle and day after day spews out, pretty much like the chain of sausages from the previous paragraph.

If you wanted your life to be, say, 'confident' and 'positive', what ingredients would you need to put in (remember, pork in/pork out, veggies in/veggies out)?

The truth is that it's your life, it's your 4000 weeks, and therefore they're your ingredients. There are too many people standing at the wrong end of the sausage machine of life. They're safely positioned at the sausages end, watching life unfold and waiting and waiting, and hoping and hoping that a good sausage will arrive.

These people will die waiting.

Kool Rule 5 suggests you'd be much better off positioning yourself at the ingredients end of life. Taking personal responsibility means you have to point the finger back at yourself and ask *what ingredients do I need to put in to make my life extraordinary?*

The truth is very simple. You can put whatever you want into the sausage machine of life.

Here's an experiment you should try. For the next two days, put 'can't be bothered', 'negativity', 'grumbling' and 'nightmare' into your life and see what happens. Then, for the two days after that, change the ingredients. Try sticking a combo of 'positivity', 'confidence', 'happiness' and 'zest' into your sausage machine.

Monitor the results. How do you feel? How much energy do you have? What are you like to be around? What results are you getting?

If the first two days of negativity get you the perfect result, go with those. If the awesome ingredients win, go with those.

It boils down to these three questions:

1. Am I going to be powerful or powerless?
2. Am I going to be a giver or taker?
3. In terms of Kool Rule 5, am I going to be a waiter or creator?

The law of the sausage machine says it's up to you.

Your choice!

Kool Rule 6 – You are the arrowhead of humanity

The mental health stats are going the wrong way. A hundred years ago 1 in 10,000 folk were depressed. Post-World War 2 it was 1 in 1000, rising to 1 in 100 in the 1970s.

Nowadays? 1 in 4.

Projecting 20 years hence, it will be rare to find anyone NOT on meds. The mentally healthy will be statistical anomalies at the end of the bell curve. The bell ends. The happy few.

Weirdos.

Remember, today's 1 in 4 are the diagnosed! The percentage feeling anxious on a regular basis is probably closer to 4 in 4. The frenetic toll of busyness weighs heavy.

For those interested in the history of mental illness (basically nobody except Dr Andy) there's a huge handbook called DSM5 (Diagnostic and Statistical Manual of Mental Disorders 5th Edition) that lists all the psychological disorders so far invented. It's the shrinks' bible.

Edition 1 listed 22 mental disorders. The latest incarnation has 297, with a lot of the disorders having an array of sub-categories.

Let's just take one, as an example. Paul Simon sang about 50 ways to leave your lover. If he was to read DSM5 he could pen a sure-fire modern hit called '37 ways to scare yourself shitless'. The DSM actually breaks anxiety down into 37 subsections. Yes, it's official, there are 37 different ways to worry.

Digging around in the mire, I discover that anxiety was only introduced into the DSM in 1980.

#WTF?

So nobody was anxious before 1980? A panic attack in 1979 was not a thing at all.

Now it's an industry.

Doesn't that beg the question, what the fuck's happened since 1980 that has caused us all to panic? Was it Duran Duran or Nena's 99 red balloons? What changed on New Year's Eve 1979? What's causing 37 different types of stress?

Stress has gone rogue.

We are a race of worriers. Worrying is in your genes. Eckhart Tolle calls it the pain body – the thinking of all humanity, passed down through the generations.

It's sobering to realize you are the arrowhead of human evolution. You are the result of a million generations of humans who managed to survive long enough to have sex. An unbroken chain of shagging. Holy moly, if that chain had been broken just once you wouldn't exist. You are the best that evolution can currently do.

Yes, YOU!

Think of all the love, passion, effort, births, near deaths, narrow escape from wolves, fevers, plagues, wars and associated scrapes that all your ancestors have experienced – ever – and they went through all that, so that you can exist.

Today.

In this moment!

The big question that we're not going to dare to ask is, were you worth it?

The big answer to the big question that we didn't just ask is, absolutely!

You are amazing. You are unique.

Congratulations. You are the arrowhead of humanity.

Therefore, it makes sense to fly high and point the way.

Kool Rule 7 – Shit happens. But not as often as you might imagine

There are hordes of what we call 'the re-animated', buzzed into life by caffeine, energy drinks and sugar. It's easy to be one of the re-animated, a sort of Frankenstein figure, hulking stiffly through your day, scaring the kids with your growling demeanour.

'Re-animated?' We're advising that you drop the 're'.

Just plain 'animated' is much better. Preferably in full colour. Brought to life by the magnificence of being able to wake up, rub the sleep from your eyes and engage with the miracle of existing on a planet with a breathable atmosphere, Coca-Cola and great music.

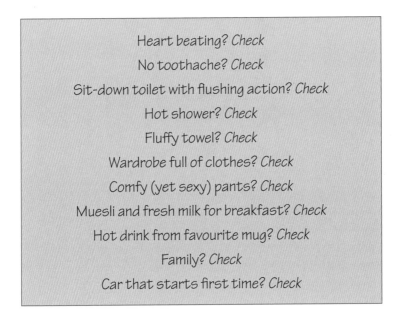

Heart beating? *Check*

No toothache? *Check*

Sit-down toilet with flushing action? *Check*

Hot shower? *Check*

Fluffy towel? *Check*

Wardrobe full of clothes? *Check*

Comfy (yet sexy) pants? *Check*

Muesli and fresh milk for breakfast? *Check*

Hot drink from favourite mug? *Check*

Family? *Check*

Car that starts first time? *Check*

You get my drift. Gratitude is like fertilizer for happiness. It's one of the quickest wins, the smallest and simplest of happiness hacks. Full colour animation costs nothing other than a modicum of energy to rethink your thinking until gratitude is grooved in.

So here's our alternative way to gratitude. Think of it as gratitude, reverse engineered.

'What hasn't happened that you didn't want that you haven't celebrated' is a mighty cool question. You can read it half a dozen times and still not get it.

While it's true that shit happens, it's also true that there's a gargantuan heap of shit that *doesn't* happen.

Hang in there. Let me explain.

Back to the question: *what hasn't happened that you didn't want that you haven't celebrated?*

We know it still hasn't sunk in so let's give you an example from full technicolour kiddie land. Children have an ability to take this to the next level. They don't need it explaining, they just get it. The first time I ever tried it was with an overexcited group of 6–8-year-olds. I gave them one minute to come up with their best examples of *what hasn't happened that you didn't want that you haven't celebrated?*

They didn't need a minute – 600 hands went ramrod straight. Half the kids were standing in an effort to make their hand the highest. The roving mic went to a six-year-old boy to my middle left. 'What hasn't happened that you didn't want that you haven't celebrated?' I asked.

The audience hushed. 'I haven't been murdered in cold blood by a ventriloquist's dummy wearing a clown costume,' he boomed.

As a presenter, this is beyond your wildest dreams. It exceeds what you could ever think of yourself and it changes the rules of the game. There's a buzz in the room. I asked him to repeat it and he did so, this time changing the emphasis so it sounded like I was an idiot for it never having crossed my mind before.

To reiterate. The lad was six.

'And did you want to be murdered by a ventriloquist's dummy?' I asked.

'Of course not,' he said. 'Especially not one dressed as a clown.' And in a sentence that brought the house down he said, 'I'll be celebrating it from now on.'

And that's the learning right there ladies and gents. From now on that lad's going to wake up punching the air in sheer delight at NOT having his throat slit by a demonic dummy.

Translated for adults, there's an awful lot of bad stuff that could have happened to you today, and hasn't.

It's weird, for sure. But noticing this stuff and celebrating its absence will tilt your brain towards positivity.

Kool Rule 8 – You're condemned to forever live in a place called 'now'

Such a wonderful rule. We'll come back to it later. Which is ironic, because the actual rule suggests that 'later' doesn't exist.

Eh?

The rule says you live in a perpetual 'now'. Which you do.

So when we return to this theme again – *later* – that will be your new 'now'.

WTF?

Kool Rule 9 – Good news is NOT news

I've got a lot of time for moths. Isn't it amazing that they can't resist the light, whereas humans are magnetically drawn to the darkness? A motorway crash delays us for hours. It's almost never the debris that causes the delay. The crash was southbound but the bigger delay's northbound, slowing down so we can gawp at the carnage. Then the traffic clears and we put our foot down, cursing the rubberneckers, without ever fully realizing we are one.

I read recently that Snow White has been banned in some schools. I'm curious, so I click. Is it some sort of politically correct dwarfism issue? Nope. It's that the Prince stole a kiss off her while she was asleep. I mean, it's a jolly good job she woke up when she did otherwise we'd have had an 18-certificate necrophiliac Disney debacle.

The point is that I clicked. I feel ashamed and dirty for doing so, hood-winked into a world of fake news where one parent in one school has made a noise, and that noise reverberates back into society in a deafening crescendo of what's called 'outrage porn'.

We're snared by clickbait. As long-established newspapers fold around us by the dozen, journalists and professional commentators have been forced to face an unpleasant truth: they're only worth the clicks they muster. In order to keep your job you have to attract an audience which attracts the advertisers. Clicks mean prizes.

And what attracts clicks?

Bile, anger, negativity, controversy. That's what.

So has Snow White actually been banned? Has 'Baa, Baa, Blacksheep' really been blacklisted? Are British kids genuinely not allowed to play conkers anymore? Is the EU truly insisting on straight bananas?

Who knows? Moreover, who fucking cares?

We have laws in the UK that mean news has to be unbiased, so we get even-handed political debate. But, of course, the news is hugely biased – towards negativity. The cheerful side of the news coin is rarely 'heads up'. These things happen every day but the headlines are never seen:

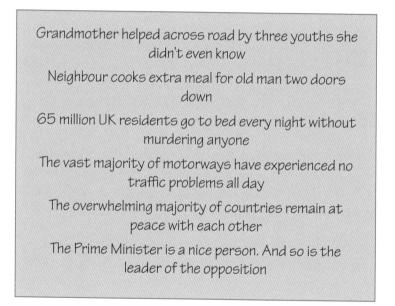

Grandmother helped across road by three youths she didn't even know

Neighbour cooks extra meal for old man two doors down

65 million UK residents go to bed every night without murdering anyone

The vast majority of motorways have experienced no traffic problems all day

The overwhelming majority of countries remain at peace with each other

The Prime Minister is a nice person. And so is the leader of the opposition

In psychology, bad weighs more than good. That means negative emotion sells far more papers than positive emotion. Angry people buy newspapers. Click-worthy headlines make money. The news stirs up an emotional response which causes us to hold a rally, with angry banners, which ends in tear gas, which feeds tomorrow's news. So tomorrow's news and radio phone-ins are basically the violence, angst and inflammation caused by today's headlines.

It's a game that you have to opt out of. So a deliciously simple top tip is to reduce your news consumption. You don't have to cut it out entirely. Consume enough so you broadly know who we're at war with, and why.

But don't marinate yourself in it.

Kool Rule 10 – You will forget all this at birth

Doh! This 10th one is a real bummer! All these cool rules and all this wisdom. And you contract a big dose of Wisdom Alzheimer's.

But the forgetfulness rule explains a lot. Rule #1 is why you focus on the bits of your body that you *don't* like. Rule #3 is why you sometimes send negative Tweets. Rule #10 is why you're shouting at the TV newsreader, #8 is why you moan about the worst part of your day, and as for the damn sausage machine! That explains why you've been waiting and waiting and waiting for life to get epic – you've been at the wrong chuffin' end!

You've been waiting instead of creating!

Rule #10 also has huge connotations for the genre of personal development.

Beyond HUGE!

It means personal development is dead in the water.

Personal *remembering*, that's where it's at.

So if rules 1 to 10 are programmed to slip your mind, we think it's worth adding one more.

Kool Rule 11 – Get bothered

And by bothered we mean *properly* bothered.

Living fully matters. Being alive matters. Kindness matters. Work matters. Relationships matter. Making a difference matters. Unpredictable naughtiness matters. Enjoying your life – starting right now – that matters most of all.

There's a global shortage of positivity, enthusiasm, happiness, optimism, hope and 'can-do' attitudes. It's more difficult to be positive than negative and, because it takes a tad more effort and a bit of practice, most people can't be bothered.

So, the 'rules' state that you'll forget 1 to 10. That leaves rule number 11 to remember and put into practice.

Know what? Upping your levels of botheredness is not a bad place to start.

Kool Rules 4 Life, in all their Tweetable glory:

1. You will receive a body
2. You will be presented with lessons
3. Haters gonna hate
4. Plot twists are coming whether you want them or not
5. Life is a sausage machine
6. You are the arrowhead of humanity
7. Shit happens. But not as often as you might imagine
8. You're condemned to forever live in a place called 'now'
9. Good news is NOT news
10. You will forget all this at birth

Which leaves this one ...

11. *Get bothered.*

Part 5
THE SCIENCEY BIT

You're often told to dig deep, find your inner strength.

Warning, if you dig too deep you'll sever a major artery.

Based on a Tweet by @PhilipArdagh

A Bump in the Night

Dr Andy's introducing his science in a mo. Before that, let's give it some context by introducing it non-scientifically and in a manner that, quite frankly, says it a whole lot better.

Gav, over to you …

Life is bursting with lovely, heart-warming moments. But let's not dodge the truth. It can also be full on, terrifying and at times scary as fuck.

Let me tell you about the most hair-raising moment of my entire life. On 16th April 2011, I arrived home from work to find my wife in labour. Don't worry, that's not the scary part, I knew she was pregnant.

The contractions had only just begun two minutes before I walked through the door. This would be our second child and with our first child taking 25 hours to appear, I figured I had a few hours' leeway.

I called the hospital to give them the update and they routinely told me to keep an eye on her and update them if anything changes or speeds up.

Just as I hung up the phone my wife's waters broke. I picked the phone right back up, called the hospital and again they told me to hang fire and keep an eye on things.

Keep an eye on things? I was mopping amniotic fluid off the kitchen floor!

Instinct kicked in. I bundled Ali into the car (carefully), handed her a Mars bar (crucial advice right there), grabbed the digestives (more important advice) and headed for the hospital.

Of course, it had to be 5:35 p.m. on a Wednesday evening. In Edinburgh city centre.

Edinburgh traffic doesn't move particularly fast at the best of times, but at peak time with many a cyclist and a few trams thrown in for good measure, it is particularly slow. Add in the potential arrival of an Oattes child and, well, we have a moment never to be forgotten.

It was now 5:45 p.m. and we were literally at a standstill. Ali was doing what all women do, being awesome. I was doing what all men do, trying to remain calm and appear like I'm not shitting myself.

I was shitting myself. On a scale of 1–10 for shitting oneself, I had shat to 11.

'I CAN FEEL THE HEAD,' screamed Ali.

My world at this point seemed to go into slow motion.

My thought process went as follows …

Can I deliver a baby?

I used to watch Casualty fairly regularly in the 90s. And I once sat through an episode of *Call the Midwife*, so, technically, yes. *Probably?* In the back of the car we had a towel and some water, how hard can it be … right? Already you can probably sense I wasn't thinking 100% clearly. In my mind I was now a midwife. I was becoming Jenny Agutter.

'THE BABY'S COMING *NOOOOW*,' screamed Ali.

Just at this moment I saw a large police van driving towards us. I leapt out of the car and stood right in the way of it. This time I *was* Jenny Agutter, but younger, and in movie form. I waved, two handed, maniacally.

The cop van screeched to a halt and the male officer who was in the driving seat asked me what was wrong.

'My wife is in the car and she's having a baby, RIGHT NOW!'

He sighed and rolled his eyes. Literally, I couldn't believe it! My world at this point seemed to go into slow motion once again.

My thought process went as follows …

Did he just sigh and roll his eyes? Yes he did, but I'm now a midwife, we're all going to be just fine.

Again, not thinking particularly clearly …

All of a sudden the female officer in the passenger seat leant over and asked, 'What did you just say?'

I replied, 'My wife is having a baby. *RIGHT FUCKING NOW!'*

Then came my favourite bit.

She smacked the male officer across the chest, put both hands in the air and yelled, 'LET'S DO THIS!'

What followed next was all a bit of a blur but it consisted of blue lights, a siren and a traffic jam that parted like the red sea. With a police escort we arrived just in the nick of time and by 6 p.m. my daughter Ellis arrived like a horse from an open stable door.

Child 1: 25 hours of labour

Child 2: 25 minutes of labour (that's another lesson, right there!)

What I learned in this moment is that there are two types of people when faced with a terrifying or stressful situation. We met both that day.

There's Keith, our male officer. And there's Hilary, our female officer.

Keith rolled his eyes. I'm sure he is a lovely man, but he rolled his eyes. A baby was coming into the world AND HE ROLLED HIS FUCKING EYES.

Hilary punched the air with two hands and shouted, 'Let's do this!'

All through life we meet Keiths and Hilarys. In every situation life throws at us we get to make a choice in the moment.

I choose never to roll my eyes.

NEVER

be an
eye roller

I choose Hilary!

So while Gav takes a breather, it's been decided that this can be Dr Andy's chapter. Sit back and enjoy the science of Hilary.

And, indeed, Keith.

Uncommon Sense

Here's how the whole of academia works. Really clever people – leaders in their field – build a body of knowledge that pushes the boundaries of what we already know. It's a never-ending game of whack-a-mole. An academic will publish their paper and go through what's called 'peer review' where the other academics beat the shit out of what you've said, before eventually popping up with a paper of their own.

And this goes on and on in an endless cycle of whack-a-mole academic one-upmanship. As a result, the subject inches forward.

Psychology is no different. Since it was invented as a subject area (the first psychology lab opened in 1879), white coated boffins have been beavering away on reams of fantastic research, proving and disproving, trying things out, gathering data, tweaking their theories, experimenting, writing papers, concocting remedies, therapies, interventions and medications, all aimed at easing suffering.

And here's the thing. Despite their very best efforts, the mental *ill*-health stats have gone the wrong way. Remember the 37 ways to worry from earlier? These are all 'official', hence researched, documented and diagnosable.

We're inventing illnesses faster than we're curing them.

So, if levels of suffering have spiked, what's a caring profession supposed to do other than work harder? Much bloody harder. Train and recruit more psychologists and mental health professionals. More pills for more people. More appointments. More therapists, counsellors and specialist hospital wings. Let's double the mental health budget. No, scrub that, this shit's really bad – let's quadruple it.

If you hover above the problem and look down on it, psychology is like a swarm of flies with the bluest arses ever. And the solution to the burgeoning problem? *Do exactly the same, but faster.*

Here's something I've never admitted before – I've been radicalized.

And I'd like to radicalize you too.

It all starts with a new word, 'metanoia', the process of experiencing a psychotic 'breakdown' and subsequent, positive psychological rebuilding or 'healing'.

In short, metanoia is a shift of mind. It's transformative.

Dick Fosbury did it. He was radicalized. Dick looked at how everybody else scissor kicked their way over a 5-foot high jump and did it differently – *backwards* – Fosbury flopping over at 7 foot 4.

Yes, I said *backwards*!

The Swedish speeding system has been experimenting with another example of metanoia. Speeders get tickets, as per normal, but those within the limit are entered into a lottery draw with prizes funded by the speeders. Drivers slow down because they want a chance of winning the lottery, whereas the real lottery winners are all those people who would normally be flattened on zebra crossings. It's a win-win-win situation.[1]

And let me throw a third example at you. A genius one: *suitcases.*

If you're over 50, think back to your first ever holiday. You will have needed suitcases. And what *didn't* those suitcases have?

Wheels!

Yes, that's right. *Actual wheels! Round things, that neolithic people invented.*

If you're under 50 years of age you'll be thinking, *No way! Really? You actually had to carry your heavy luggage?*

Yes dear reader, you lugged suitcases around by hand because nobody had thought of teaming 'luggage' with 'wheels'. Think

---

[1] I did attempt to sell this idea to my local constabulary. I even got as far as a meeting. Apparently it'll never work here. I left, amicably, suggesting it never will unless someone gives it a go. Our system continues to scissor kick at a very low height.

about it and let it sink in. The wheel is hardly a new invention. Neither is luggage.

And yet it is only in my lifetime that somebody put two and two together in a blinding flash of the bleedin' obvious. That's metanoia, a shift. It's transformative.

Transformation can happen on a personal basis. It's quite a wowza moment to step into a bright new you that you didn't know was available.

It can also happen to entire subject areas. Every so often a whole body of knowledge is cracked open and we step into a shiny new realm of possibilities.

At the back end of the last millennium, metanoia happened to psychology. Up popped *positive* psychology, flapping its fledgling wings and sidling into the limelight.

The radicalization comes from this: instead of looking at existing psychological research and whack-a-moling it, why not rethink the subject entirely and, instead of studying what's wrong with people, why not study what's right with them?

Come again?

What's *right* with people?

Cue the naysayers. *What's the point in that? Why study people who are healthy, bouyant and smiley? We've got ill people to study. Happy people? It'd be a waste of time and money because they're not ill …*

And that's the exact point, right there.

They're not ill!

The whack-a-mole psychology crowd have spent 130 years studying those who are suffering – but what about those who aren't? That handful of people you can think of, right now, who are flourishing. The happy ones. The smilers. With energy, optimism, enthusiasm and vivacity.

Yes, the exact ones that psychology has never studied. What about doing some research on them?

This had me reflecting on my own university studies and, oh my gosh, I realized that every single psychology lecture I ever attended had been named after an illness or disorder. I know about depression, anxiety and bulimia but zilch about happiness, optimism and healthy eating.

Note, this wasn't something that crept up on me in a *drip drip* of gradual realization. This jolted me like 10,000 volts. It immediately dawned on me that psychology had changed. Broken free. Transformed. Fosbury flopped. The wheels and the suitcase had been brought together!

It's so obvious! We've been whacking the wrong fucking moles!

I decided there and then that I wanted to be part of this brave new world.

Happiness Rules, OK

Before I introduce the 50/10/40 happiness ratio, you need to know it's one of those theories that has been whack-a-moled a lot. It popped up, got whacked about a bit, disappeared, popped up again.

I like it because it's simple, and it's presented as a pie (see Figure 5.1). And I like pie. So here goes:

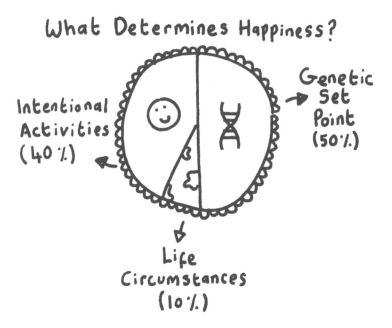

Figure 5.1 The Happiness Pie.

Taking the big wedge first, it seems that 50% of your total happiness is down to your genes, so if you've got smiley parents you have a good baseline. The word on the academic street is that you can't do much about this portion of your happiness – it's fixed.[2]

Examining the skinny 'life circumstances' portion of the happiness pie, evidence suggests that 10% of an individual's happiness is determined by factors that constitute the background of their life.

Hence your gender, ethnicity, traumas, triumphs, marital status, education level, health, income, physical appearance and your lifestyle – they matter, but not nearly as much as you think they do.

---

[2] Personally, having studied the research, I think this is nonsense. But in the interests of keeping the peace, I'll leave it be.

I know, it doesn't sound quite right, but it is. The world you live in only accounts for a measly 10%. The point is that by changing your outside circumstances you can influence 10% of your happiness and yet that's the sliver that we focus most of our efforts on. We go to extraordinary lengths to create an external lifestyle that makes us happy.

The remaining 40% of an individual's happiness – the 'intentional activities' section of the pie – is directly under our control. It is this sizeable chunk of happiness that gives us scope to raise our levels in the here and now.

Let me put it even more bluntly. I spent the best part of 12 years seeking out and interviewing happy people. But it only took about 2 weeks to realise they've got the same shit in their life that I have. Happy people live in the same world as me. EXACTLY the same world. It rains on them. They get stuck in traffic jams. Their workplace announces a restructure every few months. They get speeding tickets. They can't find a car parking space. Their elderly relatives have dementia, same as mine.

And yet they still manage to be happy.

To be crystal clear about this, a massive chunk of your happiness – 40% or more – can be influenced by changing what's going on *inside* your head.

And here's where it gets super interesting – create the life that you want from the inside out. Do that first and you're more likely to create an external world that works for you.

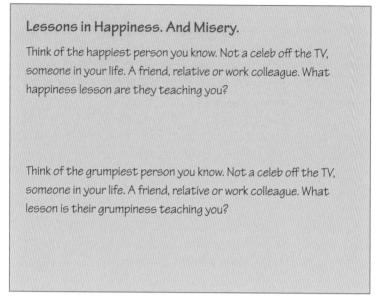

Lessons in Happiness. And Misery.

Think of the happiest person you know. Not a celeb off the TV, someone in your life. A friend, relative or work colleague. What happiness lesson are they teaching you?

Think of the grumpiest person you know. Not a celeb off the TV, someone in your life. A friend, relative or work colleague. What lesson is their grumpiness teaching you?

Having an *In-sperience*

The story so far … pretty much forever, psychology has been predicated on the question, *how can we alleviate suffering?*

The answer that's been doggedly pursued is this: *you have to identify people who are struggling, find out why and fix them.*

Just to be absolutely clear, I'm not dissing traditional forms of psychology. They remain valid, useful and life-changing. It's not about tearing up the rule book or suggesting disorders aren't disorders. Those 37 types of worry? I might be a bit sceptical but, hey, someone's done some clinical research so I'll go with it. Schizophrenia is still schizophrenia and a bout of anxiety is still anxiety. If you're experiencing a full-blown panic attack, that feels very real indeed. If you're clinically depressed, that's really bad shit.

It boils down to this: we've been studying ill people to find a cure for illness. But what if happy people have got the cure? What if they *are* the cure? There are a rush of questions that I'd never considered: Who are the happy people, what are happy people doing to be so happy and, most crucially of all, what can we learn from them that we can apply to our own lives, so we can join them?

Rather than studying folk with ailments and inventing disorders to label them and remedies to cure them, wouldn't it be ace to a study people with zestful vigour and smiley faces who, to this point in history, have been shunned by the psychology profession on the grounds of 'not being ill'?

So I decided to seek out the zestful few rather than the troubled many.

For proper academics my thesis is available at www.artofbrilliance. co.uk. Yes, all 130,000 words of it. The science of happy people. Go whack-a-mole it if you want.

For everyone else, here's the headline news version.

If, this week, you kept a diary of your emotions and we plotted the results on a graph, you'd have an upper and lower level. So, in a normal week, you will live your life between these two limits of upper level 'feel good' and lower level 'feel lousy'.

Straight away, this is oversimplified. You can have *extreme* ups and downs, hence you can go higher than your 'normal' high (aka 'mania', characterized by super-high energy, racing thoughts, fast talking, high sex drive, irritability and aggression) and lower than your 'normal' low (a depressive episode, characterized by low energy, emptiness, loneliness, lack of sex drive, in fact lack of interest in anything).

I'm not talking about the extremes. If you're experiencing a very low low or a very high high, or are oscillating between the two, you should make an appointment with your doctor. Seriously.

I'm talking about you, on a *normal* week, existing between your *normal* emotional tolerance levels. Feeling amazing at one end and feeing lousy at the other.

Plotting my data on a graph, the screaming tabloid headline would be this: *most people are a million miles away from feeling as great as they could.*

I describe it as the curse of mediocrity. To clarify, I'm not talking about being depressed. Most people are just a bit stuck in ways of thinking and behaving that makes life a bit bland. We're huffing and puffing our way through our days. Often, it's born from low-level exhaustion brought on by the manic pace of this crazy millennium.

Positive psychology acknowledges the inevitability of emotional down time, while also attempting to provide strategies to minimize it. So while clinical psychology has always been useful to those most in need, positive psychology is applicable to us all.

Why? Because EVERYONE wants to be happier. Even really happy people want to be happier! It's the most sought after feeling on the planet. Plus, you don't just want it for yourself, it's what you want most for your children. Yes, sending them to school and being conversant with Macbeth or understanding the basics of an isosceles triangle is all well and good but what I really want for my own offspring is that they live happy lives.

End of.

Despite it being the world's number one wish, it's actually quite easy to get stuck in an emotional no-man's land, a sticky ambivalence of 'fair to middling'. If you stop, look and listen, you'll find it's very common. We just love to fit in so it's easy to slip into doing the same as everyone else.

'Fair to middling' can become your norm.

'Sometimes you're the windshield; sometimes you're the bug.'

Mark Knopfler

My academic interest has been piqued by the 2%ers, my pet name for the small but perfectly formed coalition of happiness outliers, the non-ill, flourishing few who reside at the upper end of the emotional graph. They are statistical oddballs who are not only happier and more energized in themselves but who also raise the levels of optimism and energy in those around them. In short, they're good to have around – at work and at home. Shunned by the psychology profession on the grounds of 'not being ill' but warmly embraced by me for *exactly the same reasons.*

2%er

You will know one or two; the handful of people who you can think of in your life who, when they're around, you feel good too. Leakage. Emotional spillage. Those who create upward spirals of emotion. These were the people I was looking for.

The ultra-quick win is to understand that happiness is less about what's going on around you and more about your internal processing of those events. Yes dear reader, your starting point is to understand that happiness is an inside job.

Happiness is not an ex-perience, it's an in-sperience. That's basically it!

And herein also lies its problem. I adore the subject. Positive psychology has changed my life. It has established itself as a proper bona fide science, as in we go to great lengths to gather data, test theories, bend and break what we know, and yet the results are often really obvious.

In trying to establish itself as a 'proper' subject (and not to be seen as a wishy-washy positive thinking 'Pollyanna riding a unicorn over a rainbow' kind of thing) positive psychology has had to steroid up. To risk not having sand kicked in its face it's had to cloak itself in academic language. Whereas, of all the strands of psychology, it's the one that needs less oil and less of the gym. It has life-enhancing properties and therefore needs to be accessible.

To everyone.

Remember, the inaccessible version is available on my website. Here's the plain simple English version. My findings, combined with oodles of other good stuff that I've garnered along the way. No steroids. No oiled-up six-pack or bulging biceps.

It doesn't need all that claptrap because underneath it all, positive psychology is a beautiful thing.

The Chase

Recently I did a training session for some brand new soon-to-be teachers. The aim was to get them shipshape and inspection-ready, as they were about to embark on their classroom voyage.

Bright-eyed and bushy-tailed?

Erm, no. Exhausted. Haggard. Drawn. Weary. Pale. *Yes.*

Several had been warned off the profession by staff they'd met along the way. Actual teachers. The ones counting down till half term, summer, retirement and then, presumably, death.

Our newbies had heard tales of it being 'better in the old days' and I nodded, as sagely as I could, before explaining that that might or might not be true. Either way, those olden days are gone. If we're hanging on all misty-eyed to how it used to be we're going to struggle in the new days. Because the new days are different. Kids are different. The workload is different. Expectations are different.

And therefore we need to be different.

Think about it for a second. These teachers haven't even finished their training – they are not actually teachers yet – and they're already looking forward to the summer holidays.

It's called 'destination addiction'. Teachers get it pretty bad, but everyone suffers to some extent.

Brace yourself. This is massive.

'Happiness' has been sold to you as a fantastic pot of emotional gold, buried at the end of the rainbow. It's a wonderful feeling that you want more of and it's 'over there'. Happiness is the reward, the X-marks-the spot treasure that we all crave. It's something you must earn, or pursue.

The chase is on. Always.

This way of thinking has been drummed into you (and we're about to drum it out). Reflecting on your school days, your parents and teachers tell you that if you work hard at primary school you'll get great SATs results. And when you get those great results, guess what? Then you'll be happy.

And they will have told you that if you work hard at big school you'll get great GCSEs and then you'll be happy. Am I right? Or am I right?

And you'll get a job and you'll be happy. And then you'll get married and be happy.

You are sold the vision of 'I'll be happy when … '

In terms of tweaking your thinking, what if that's a big fat lie? What if it all works the other way around, so 'happiness' *is* a fantastic feeling – a pot of emotional gold at the end of the rainbow – but what if it's at this end?

What if being happy NOW is the key to success. The rules change dramatically once you realize happiness is the starting point, not the ending point. It's no wonder we can't find happiness because – the big fat 'X-marks-the-spot' – we're fucking standing on it!

Working through the previous examples, what if it's the happiest kids that get the best results? What if it's the happiest employee getting the promotion, what if being happy now is the key to finding your perfect partner because, let's face it, you're much more attractive when you're smiling.

What if we've been looking for happiness in exactly the wrong place?

Humans have what psychologists call a 'set point', a kind of happiness thermostat which, in the UK, hovers around the 7 out of 10 mark. This set point acts as a kind of emotional elastic band, dragging you back to feeling *mildly happy most of the time*. It also explains why lottery winners have a temporary rise in happiness before the effect wears off and they too settle back to the point of 'same happiness but bigger house'.

Mildly happy most of the time is not a bad place to be. It's certainly a whole lot better than *clinically depressed for all of the time*.

But if you're determined to squeeze the max out of life, your happiness bar needs to be raised.

> ### Torschlusspanik. German
>
> *'Gate-closing panic'*: the worry/fear about diminishing life opportunities as one gets older; also refers to people acting hastily generally when time is running out.

The next chapter is your brain's re-wiring exercise.

Neurological Fosbury Flopping.

Read on. It'll give you stickability.

Contagion?

Emotions are viral. Your emotional system is open – in Wi-Fi terms, everyone can log onto your signal and you can log onto theirs. So when you're feeling great, other people will catch that feeling. If you're having a stinker, guess what, you're contaminating those around you with bad stuff.

The brain-to-brain link creates an emotional bond, thus affecting your biology. The openness of your emotional system, the fact that we're hard-wired to catch other people's feelings, means that we create one another. Let me say that again, so it sinks in a bit better – your emotions not only affect you and the chemical composition of *your* body, they also transmit to those around you, creating *that* person in *that* moment.

It works via mirror neurons which means we're compelled to copy others' emotions and behaviours. These mirror neurons allow contagion, letting the feelings we witness flow through us, thus helping us get in synch with the person feeling the emotion. This ability to 'feel' with and for them is the basis of empathy.

It's a super-sophisticated form of subconscious communication. Daniel Goleman nails it, concluding that our nervous systems 'are constructed to be captured by the nervous systems of others, so we can experience others as if it was from within their skin'. So, at an unconscious level we are in constant unspoken dialogue with everyone we interact with.

Remember, humans are constructed with this emotional openness. You cannot NOT have an impact.

Hence the bit when you come home from work is crucial. The concept of 'para-sympathetic arousal' means that your family will catch your emotions. In a bizarre tradition, many families go through a ritual of offloading all their emotional baggage on the ones they love most in life.

If this habit occurs day after day, it has a cumulative effect on family well-being. Negative emotions work a bit like second-hand smoke – you catch them whether you want to or not. Also, it's not just the inevitability of the transfer, there's also a flavour. Goleman calls it 'emotional soup'; the concept that, in any social situation, everyone is adding a certain 'flavour' to the prevailing atmosphere.

Two things spring to mind. First, dare to ask yourself what flavour you are adding. Are you coming through the door with joy and enthusiasm or are you poisoning the family atmosphere with toxicity? And, second, not all family members are equal. Yes, everyone is adding something to the emotional soup but, as a parent, you are adding the most. For 'parent' read 'leader without a title' – your emotional contagion is massive. Please note, I am not pontificating about you finding your impact or experimenting with it; I am screaming that you are already having it. This is a less than gentle reminder for you to wield your impact in a positive way.

Christakis and Fowler report that a happy friend makes you 25% happier (but only if they live within a mile of you). A happy sibling raises your happiness by 14% and a happy neighbour raises your happiness by a whopping 34%.

There's more. Your 'emotional spillage' creates a ripple effect that reaches 3 degrees of people removed from you. On a good day your positivity bubbles over, creating an uplift in those around you. Bottom line? You, in TGI Monday mode, are positively impacting on your friends, your friends' friends, and your friends' friends' friends.

If we apply the ripple effect to a simple situation – say, the workplace – you coming in full of genuine enthusiasm and positivity will resonate with your work colleagues. They will experience an upward spiral of emotions simply because you're in their life.

But it doesn't stop there. Your work colleagues then go home to their families and because they're feeling great, their family is now benefiting from your positivity.

But it doesn't stop there either! One of those family members pops out to the supermarket and has some banter with the lady on the checkout and she's now feeling more positive.

Just to be clear, you haven't met your work colleagues' family or the lady on the checkout, but all of those people are feeling amazing because of you. Your joie de vivre has leaked!

Your superpowers of positivity work remotely and invisibly.

It boils down to this – you're contagious. Be careful what you spread!

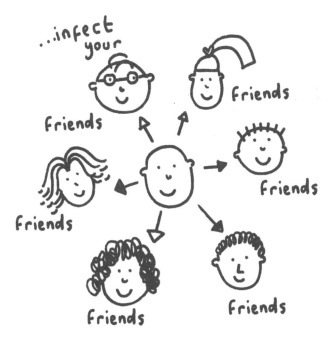

Part 6
SILENCE OF THE LAMBS

> **Weird World**
>
> 'One of the main aims is to be followed by as many strangers as possible.'
>
> *A parent explaining Twitter to their child.*

Phake Fobias

Welcome to our technology chapter.

Thankfully, we don't actually know anything about technology, so we'll make it brief and hard-hitting.

It might be wise to adopt the brace position; there's passion afoot.

Before we get to actual tech stuff, there's something you need to know about your brain. It's sold to you as a wonderful piece of kit, a miracle of evolution (or God?) that somehow creates consciousness and thought.

But what nobody ever tells you is that your brain is also a lying bastard, full of half-truths, best guesses and blatant fabrication. It's a 3-pound jello con artist.

Your brain makes sense of the world and to do so it makes things up. It's a best guesser. Dan Gilbert describes the human brain as an 'anticipation machine'. If you hear a snippet of news or gossip, it immediately fills in the blanks for you. It finds it very easy to create false memories so, for example, when scientists expose people to Photoshopped images of themselves at various events years prior, they were soon able to explain what they were doing and recall the event with clarity even though they were never there.

See what I mean? The lying bastard! It takes snippets of vision, sounds, taste, touch and smell and matches them with your memory banks to weave its version of what you call reality.

Gilbert calls it 'nexting': your brain is continually moving onto the next thing and it is especially keen for the 'nexts' to fit a pattern. So the sentence 'The cat sat on the …' means your brain automatically chooses a word to fit the pattern it expects. In fact it guesses, arriving at an answer milliseconds *before* it gets to the word. And while it's guessing correctly, your brain keeps scanning this book, left to right, down and down the page until, 'and they all lived happily ever … pineapple' stops you in your tracks. It's only when your brain predicts badly that you suddenly feel bacon sandwich.

Let's take vision as an example. Your eyes are detecting waves of light which register in your head and your wonderful brain constructs an image of what it thinks is *just about right.* I know that sounds (and looks and feels) ridiculous but I promise you that huge chunks of your vision are made up – constructed, fabricated – your brain giving you its best guess of what's out there. At best, 10% of what you see is actually what is there. The other 90%? Your brain fills in the blanks according to what it thinks is probably there.

I know you're unconvinced, so try this:

Cover your left eye and with your right eye look at the X below. Then, slowly, move the page towards you. At some point before your nose touches the page the X will disappear. That blind spot has been there your whole life. Usually your brain effortlessly fills in this gap for you.

X

This is but a tiny example of a much bigger point.

There's a whole load of totally made up stuff that you couldn't make up. It's too stupid.

And this section is that.

You'll notice a creeping sense of incredulity where the furrowed brow of 'is what we're writing actually true' is gradually replaced by the Chinese water torture – the *drip drip drip* realization that, yes, it genuinely is.

Every last word is true.

Our lazy internet search reveals you can have a complex about almost anything. Here's a fun game for all the family. We're calling it 'Phake Fobia' and we're pretty sure it'll be coming to Channel 5 soon.

We've listed 10 phobias. Nine are real. Can you spot the fake one?

1. Coulrophobia: running scared of clowns.
2. Omphalophobia: terrified of belly buttons.
3. Papaphobia: shit scared of the Pope.
4. Arachibutyrophobia: panicked by the idea of peanut butter sticking to the roof of your mouth.
5. Allodoxaphobia: all aquiver over other people's opinions.
6. Oikophobia: kitchen appliances. Yes, your toaster's out to get you, the bastard.
7. Genuphobia: knees. Not necessarily knobbly ones. Just knees generally.
8. Anatidaephobia: the fear that a goose is watching you. Or a duck. And to be clear, the fear is NOT that it's attacking you. Just watching.

9. Turophobia: Fearful of feta? Chilled by cheddar? Panicked by parmesan? Turophobia is a fear of cheese.
10. Phobophobia: fear of phobias.

Obviously the first one is an actual genuine thing. Clowns! They're no laughing matter, right?

So that leaves the other nine, and it's actually quite hard to pick an odd one out because they all seem pretty stupid. Toasters? Cheese? Sticky peanut butter? They're totally irrational. That is unless you actually suffer from them, in which case they're going to affect your thinking and behaviour.

For the record, the fake one is the goose thing. It's a fake fear dreamed up by Gary Larson for his Far Side cartoons. Now this is weird, but since compiling this list I think I've developed it! Some feathery bastard is watching me, observing my every move. It's much scarier than cheese, knees or the Pontiff.

Comparisonitis

So hang on, humans have created a whole load of silly-sounding phobias. And people actually have these fears?

Yes. And it seems that stupidity is contagious. Proof? Let's check out the burgeoning cases of 'comparisonitis'.

It's safe to say we live in the age of envy. It's lush and green and ubiquitous: career envy, kitchen envy, children envy, food envy, 6-pack stomach envy, holiday envy. You name it, there's an envy for it.

We gaze at our slimming, filtered #OutfitOfTheDay, and we want that body – not the one that feels tired and bloated on the morning commute. While we're busy finding the perfect camera angle, our lives become a dazzling, flawless charade. Our defence against the dark art of everyone else's fake life is to attack, with an even faker portrait of our own existence.

Sad Fact:

Black cats languish in animal shelters because they are not 'selfie-friendly'.

Social media means envy is being taken to an extreme. We've sold our souls to consumerism; desperately seeking something. Are we chasing something out there to fill a void in here? We are, as the poet Lucretius put it a few thousand years ago, the proverbial 'sick man ignorant of the cause of his malady'.

Is wanton materialism sensible?

Actually, yes it is. If you genuinely think that your happiness depends on having more stuff or a sexier car, a better job or a holiday home in Marbella – then it makes perfect sense to chase said stuff.

Psychologists report seeing more envy in their consulting rooms. Dr Windy Dryden (actual real name) suggests that at a *logical* level we all know that images are filtered and that people are presenting the very best take on their lives, but on an *emotional* level, it's still pushing our buttons.

No age group or social class is immune, although teenage girls might have it worse than most. While envying other people is damaging enough, social psychologist Sherry Turkle (real name, again) hints at something more pernicious. Everyone else is posting the best of the best, creating an illusory 'best of' that we put out there. We then look at the lives we have constructed online and feel a fear of missing out in relation to our own lives. Basically, Dr Turkle (*still* her real name) is suggesting we don't measure up to the lives we tell others we are living. Hang in there, because here it comes in all its bare-knuckled ridiculousness – we feel envious of the fake life that we've curated.

Self-envy! We become envious of our own avatars.

Is it any surprise that we're so mentally fucked up when we're the ones generating the fucked-up-ness?

So why do we feel the need to post, share, scroll and compare?

Because that's what social creatures do.

We're social creatures.

Human beings look around at what everyone else is doing … *and copy.* As William Deresiewicz rightly points out, we become the world's most excellent sheep.

The problem with social media is that we might be copying the *wrong* behaviours.

Baaaaaa.

You've Arrived

When you drive off the ferry at New Zealand's Waiheke Island you're greeted by a sign that says 'Slow down. You're here'. What a wonderful reminder about life in general.

Because if you look around you'll see the opposite; hordes of homo sapiens grabbing the reins of the materialistic chariot and digging their spurs deep into the horse's flank. *Faster! Faster!*

The modern world is, on balance, a fabulous place. But we're burdened with excess baggage.

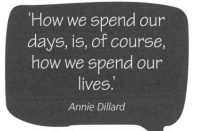

'How we spend our days, is, of course, how we spend our lives.'

Annie Dillard

We've have been taught that freedom is the freedom to pursue our petty, trivial desires. Whereas real freedom is freedom *from* our petty, trivial desires.

And there's nothing more tempting than a smartphone, a distraction device designed to lure you into idling away your time. This is okay until you twig that time is all you have. Glued to your screen, downloading your emails, watching cat videos, uploading a picture of your meal, checking your calendar, posting a Twitter update, checking your favourite websites – your life clock doesn't stop ticking as you stare at your screen.

Your life is not on pause. The cheeky 40 minutes it has taken to do all of the above – this IS your life.

The problem with the world wide web is entanglement in stimulation of the shallow kind. The bubblegum kind – scrolling, double-thumbing, updating, checking – it keeps you occupied but there is little nutritional value.

Rather than being connected, I think we're becoming more and more *dis*connected – from ourselves. The problem isn't really technology. It's emptiness and lack of focus.

Before we offer solutions I think we need to hold our hands up and admit that your author tag team is guilty too.

As Gav admits, every day for the last 10 years I've contemplated chucking my smartphone away. I hate it. I hate everything about it.

Why? Coz I CAN'T STOP LOOKING AT IT! And 99% of the time what do I see?

Nothing. Nothing that matters. Nothing important. Nothing meaningful.

Social media is the worst for this. When used well, I really believe it has its place. I'm now re-reading that last sentence – do I truly believe this? I'm beginning to think not. Maybe. Kind of. I dunno?

I looked at Facebook the other day and someone had posted the following …

'Can you believe some people?!'

That's it! What the actual fuck? Why would anyone feel the need to post this? What does it even mean? Worse still, why am I reading it?

In turn, of course, the comments posted below went as follows …

'You alright hun?'

'Call me?'

'You keep smiling babe, know who your real friends are.'

Reading the inane FB comment is bad enough and now I've gone and got myself embroiled in reading the equally banal comments. I feel grubby. Violated.

I was chatting with a friend about this recently and he told me he spends an hour a day on Facebook. I told him I thought that was crazy and his exact response was as follows …

'But what would you do instead?'

Are you kidding me?

LIVE!

That's what I'd do. *I'd live my life.*

What's that coming over the hill? Is it a monster? Yes, it's a big fat scary monster of a generation who rarely look up, who appear to prefer documenting their life rather than living it.

Examples abound. Here's one: I popped into Starbucks the other day to use the loo and on the way out spotted a group of six young people, aged about 14, sitting around a table with their Frappuccinos. Every single one sitting in silence staring at their phones. On leaving I decided to join the queue to buy a coffee and for the next 10 minutes the silence at said table continued. No one chatting, no one laughing, two doing duck faces for the camera and then they upped and left.

This might sound fairly normal nowadays but here's my question. How did they all know to leave at the same time? I asked one of them, their reply? 'Alana messaged me.'

I asked who Alana was, and she pointed at the girl beside her.

Again, let this sink in for a moment …

Now don't get me wrong, I do the social media thing and at times it can provide big entertainment, huge learning, new business, and it can even make me feel happy.

But …

If used incorrectly, it infuriates, bores, angers, stresses, and to put it bluntly makes me feel glum. Actually it makes me feel ill. Literally, there's been times I'm sitting staring, scrolling endlessly and I feel unwell.

In the *New York Times*, Matthew Crawford claims that 'We have allowed our attention to be monetized, if you want it back you're going to have to pay for it.'

Basically, attention is a limited resource. We only have so much of it and because it's a scarce resource, it's valuable. It's happened very quickly. Huge swathes of public space have been auctioned off to private commercial interests, with their constant demands on us to look at the products on display or simply absorb some bit of corporate messaging.

Withdrawing cash from a machine? Here's an advert.

Want to watch a YouTube vid? Sit through a commercial before we let you.

Long haul flight? Seat back. Get comfy. Stick a movie on the in-flight system and, behold, there's an advert.

Waiting at a bus stop? There's a scrolling ad, and when the bus turns up it's actually a huge red commuting billboard.

Crawford suggests that we've opened a new frontier of capitalism, complete with its own frontier ethic: to boldly dig up and monetize every bit of private head space by appropriating our collective attention. 'In the process, we've sacrificed silence – the condition of not being addressed. And just as clean air makes it possible to breathe, silence makes it possible to think.'

And maybe that's the point, right there. Silence makes it possible to think so no silence = no thinking. If we stopped to think things through, we'd rebel. So the modern marketeers have made sure there's no time or place to stop.

Remember when we used to go to the toilet and we'd sit and read the back of the air freshener? Not any more, we can sit and enjoy a poo while reading all about the latest holiday Debra's booked that YOU CAN'T AFFORD BUT SHE'S TELLING THE WORLD ANYWAY.

We're agitated. We're on edge. We struggle to stop, to relax, to switch off, to simply be. And in a delicious irony, we are now willing to pay for silence. We pay for mindfulness apps, meditation courses and mountain retreats.

Families watching a movie together, but mum's checking her Instagram. Couples out for a meal, just the two of them together, sitting across from each other, in love, romantically looking into their phone screens. Dad playing with his kids while scrolling and not actually paying any attention to what their child is doing. Or worse, parents handing the kids their phone at every opportunity because it's easier.

Easier than what?

Easier than playing with your kids? Easier than talking to them? Easier than inventing awesomely ridiculous games to play with them? Easier than building a den with them?

For anyone reading this feeling their blood boil because you do this and you're feeling victimized, unfairly singled out … the authors of *Zest* are big bad bullies.

Chill, I assure you our blood is boiling too as we've done all of the above.

Our detox solutions are coming. First we have to visit a section of the book where truth really is stranger than fiction. A place where we've parked everything that we literally couldn't have made up.

Please adopt the brace position. This is the graveyard slot for paragraphs that are hilariously un-funny.

GTFOSMAGO

Here's the thing. In the last 15 years, we've gone from one Bakelite house phone (with accompanying phone directory and door stop of a thing called the *Yellow Pages*) which was in the hallway, and couldn't be moved from the hallway and which we shared – to having a phone each. No wires, lives in your pocket (or in the case of my teenagers, in their actual hands), no phone book or BIG yellow book or address book where your nan's number was listed. It's not really a phone at all, it's a Swiss Army knife modern-day survival kit that does everything except everything a Swiss Army knife did.

My point is that your smartphone has become your prosthetic brain. An essential, not just for communication, but for measuring your heart rate and keeping you alive. If you toddle off to work and accidentally leave your phone at home, it's an issue, right?

It's called 'phone separation anxiety'. There's a ramped-up version called nomophobia – the fear of being without your smartphone.

No, it's not like being watched by a goose, it's an actual thing and it affects people of all ages.

Dr Kim Ki Joon commented, 'The findings of our study suggest that users perceive smartphones as their extended selves and get attached to the devices … people experience feelings of anxiety and unpleasantness when separated from their phones.'

Professor Mark Griffiths weighs in, linking it to FOMO (Fear of Missing Out). 'People don't use their phones to talk to other people – we are talking about an internet-connected device that allows people to deal with lots of aspects of their lives,' he says. 'You would have to surgically remove a phone from a teenager because their whole life is ingrained in this device.'

Griffiths thinks attachment theory, where we develop emotional dependency on the phone because it holds details of our lives, is a small part of nomophobia. For 'screenagers', it is FOMO that creates the most separation anxiety. If they can't see what's happening on Snapchat or Instagram, they become panic-stricken about not knowing what's going on socially, 'But they adapt very quickly if you take them on holiday and there's no internet,' says Griffiths.

My response to that is *you take your teenagers to somewhere with no internet?* First of all, where exactly is that 'no internet' place? You holidaying in Syria? And secondly, why? What have your kids done that's so bad to be punished with such a shockingly dull holiday?

Parking my incredulity, the top tip by the tip-top academic is this: 'Turning your phone off or leaving it at home can reduce dependency and anxiety.' I'm sure Professor Griffiths is a nice person but what's his middle name? Sherlock?

Look, I've admitted to being a bit elderly. I am of the generation where we had one phone, in the hallway. It had no apps. I'm probably not as 'with it' as some of the readers, but things are about to get really silly.

I've been doing some digging. FOMO is way old. Apparently the latest anxiety faced by social media users is MOMO (the *Mystery of Missing Out*), aka the paranoia that stems from your friends not posting anything at all. You start thinking, *are they having so much fun that they can't even share it?*

Rosie, 24, tells the *Telegraph* reporter, 'I have my favourite Instagram profiles I like to check daily. If they go quiet I get MOMO for sure.' She admits to getting stressed, worrying that they might be doing something more interesting than her. 'You think – what can be so good that they aren't posting?'

The newspaper consults a professional psychologist who explains that MOMO might be a new word but it's not a new thing. Apparently it's about being part of a peer group. Fitting in is what we do. Remember when there was a playground game and you got left out, or a party that you never got invited to?

It's that.

The professional psychologist proceeds to dispense sensitive advice to Rosie, as though MOMO is an actual major phenomenon. Our advice is less 'kid gloves' and more bare knuckled truth: Rosie, stop checking your phone so often. Get a life of your own. Stop being such a flake.

I'm struggling to comprehend the double negatives in 'BROMO' – the act of your bros (i.e. 'friends', keep up people!) not posting pictures of the party you missed, so as to avoid 'rubbing things in'.

Come again?

BROMO. You're worried that your mates *haven't* posted pics of a party you *didn't* go to?

Glad that's cleared up.

Then there's FOJI – the Fear of Joining In (the flipside to FOMO), based on the idea of opting out of Instagram and its ilk because you don't know what to post and/or you're afraid no one will follow you.

Assuming you're still reading and haven't slung the book away in frustration at people creating fake stress, there are two more that warrant a mention.

SLOMO, aka 'Slow to Miss Out'. What happens when you've checked out of social media for the night and awake to find your Instagram feed riddled with other people's fun. Imagine the horror! You're way off the pace. Day ruined. Obviously.

Soon we'll have FONKDFSHAA: The Fear Of Not Knowing Dave From School Has An Audi. Or FOFTPMSBIWDWHTFSMMTD: The Fear Of Forgetting To Post Mundane Shite Because If We Don't We'll Have To Find Something More Meaningful To Do.

What about GTFOSMAGO? Get The Fuck Off Social Media And Go Outside.

Sarcasm (and frustration) aside, we have found a modern-day social media phenomenon that we adore, JOMO, the 'Joy of Missing Out', a worthy alternative floated a couple of years ago, based on the fallacious premise that non-participation is something to be relished. It might be an age thing but JOMO is the only one I 'suffer' from.

People posting pics of uproariously drunken late parties that I've *not* gone to – that makes me happy as Larry.

Idea Factory

Ever sworn at your satnav?

Me too.

I'm thinking of inventing a happy style satnav. It'd get you to places but cheer you up along the way.

'Look, I know you've just missed the turning but look around you. What a lovely part of town to be lost in!'

'Check out the view to your left. Wowza!'

'Traffic jam! Bummer! But, hey, just be glad you're not in the accident that caused it.'

'Nearly home. I know you've had a tough day but, do you know what, I reckon you need to go through that door like the best dad in the world.'

Digi Detox

Alan Lightman claims that by not giving ourselves the minutes – or hours – free of devices and distractions, we risk losing our ability to know who we are and what's important to us.

He's spot on. It's already happening. We have teenagers more interested in collecting likes and being validated by complete strangers than going to bed. We have people of all ages unable to put their phones down when their children are telling them their daily news.

Lightman reminds us that the destruction of our inner selves via the wired world is a more recent, and subtler, phenomenon. The loss of slowness, of time for reflection and contemplation, of privacy and solitude, of silence, of the ability to sit quietly in a chair for fifteen minutes without external stimulation—all have happened quickly and almost invisibly.

A hundred and fifty years ago, the telephone didn't exist.

Thirty years ago, the internet didn't exist.

Twenty years ago, Google didn't exist.

When you log on in a hotel or cafe you get a 'username'. You're therefore a 'user'. People who shoot up on heroin, they're 'users' too.

Look, I'm not ranting or stressing, merely pointing to something that we all know is coming. This is a bigger change than any of the 'next generation' huffing and puffing that has gone before.

One of the British universities investigated compulsive gambling, internet addictions and the excessive, perhaps even dangerous, use of social networking sites. Technological compulsion like 'social media addiction' comes with all the behavioural signals that we might usually associate with chemical addictions, such as smoking or alcoholism. These include mood changes, social withdrawal, conflict and relapse.

An addiction is when you invest in an activity to the point of it becoming harmful. Drugs, alcohol, food, cigarettes – the harm is obvious and overt. Screen time is less obvious but I know people who are so engrossed in social media and/or video games that they neglect everything else in their lives.

It's hard not to ridicule the official advice for smartphone detoxing, which is to download an app that tells you how long you've been on the phone.

An app!

To detox your phone addiction, you download an app? That's like detoxing an alcoholic with a bottle of Jack Daniels!

Everything you do on your phone should be intentional.

So here are our digital detox rules:

- Sign out of each app after you've used it. This will require you to sign back in every time you try to use them again. There's not much chance you'll remember the password, hence you can't just mindlessly open them up and scroll through whenever you have a free second.
- Delete all social media apps from your phone; check these only from a desktop computer.
- Turn all banner-style/pop-up/sound notifications off.
- Leave your phone in your pocket or keep it out of sight for meetings, get-togethers, conversations and meals.
- At home, get a second fruit bowl and make it a 'phone bowl'. House rules: all visitors and residents deposit their phone in said bowl. If you want to check it, you have to go to the bowl, check and replace your phone into the bowl. It's your house, so your rules.
- Keep your phone out of sight during your commute. Watch the world go by instead. You'll see lots of people on their phones. Smile at the irony.

- Don't take your phone with you into the bathroom or toilet. In a delicious throwback, read the air freshener instead.
- Choose two hours a day to switch your phone off. And then stick to it.
- Get an old Nokia. Phone calls, texting and Snake. What more do you need?
- Get a new hobby. We suggest running. Or taxidermy. Or talking to people.
- Instead of thinking about 'spending less time on your phone', think about 'spending more time on your life'.
- Ban phones from the dinner table. Try talking to your family instead. Be sure to ask them about the highlight of their day.
- Stop being a dick.

A word about 'sharing etiquette'. There's a time and a place for sharing an experience; ideally having experienced it yourself first. If you're preoccupied with 'sharing', then the moment has already changed – the act of sharing becomes your focus. We dare you to be the one who's in the moment. The moment is enough. You were in it. You know because you were there. Nobody else needs to know. That moment. It's yours to keep.

But please be careful not to tut at the ones who are capturing everything. The ones who actually miss their 5-years-old's nativity performance in the flesh because they're too busy recording it so they can experience it on a 2-inch by 4-inch screen later. You don't need to be righteous about being right. Smug is bad. Inner peace, that's a good place to be.

It boils down to this, as a general rule of thumb, sharing stuff on social media is akin to masturbation; it's not 'wrong', but you need to be selective as to where, when, how often and with whom.

And if you overdo it, you will go blind.

Be More Pumba

In true Columbo style, just one more thing …

Phones. Hours of your life slipping by absorbed in trivia.

Comparisonitis. We don't think it's about interpreting envy as a positive or a negative, but trying to understand what it is telling you. Why are you wanting to scratch people's eyes out?

What if it's not about them? It might be a sign that you need to have a good look at yourself?

The answer is not necessarily about being more honest about our lives – it might sometimes lie in simply shutting up.

> 'Only when you drink from the river of silence shall you indeed sing.'
>
> Khalil Gibran, 'The Prophet'

Comparing yourself with yourself is where the magic sauce really is. Am I a little bit better than I was yesterday? If you can answer 'yes' to that most days, you'll be growing. We figure it's less about being the best in the world and more about being the best *for* the world. It's perfectly okay to go about that quietly and unassumingly.

Show up, do good work, be nice, hakuna matata.

Repeat.

I wonder whether the constant churn of trivia and their addiction to superficial information will keep future generations from attending to the important issues of the day?

Will the need for immediacy diminish gratitude and empathy?

Will social media keep future generations from connecting with others in a meaningful way?

Will talking become less important? Will students be writing essays in emoji language?

Our aim was to write this chapter so you can consider creating some sort of mental green belt, a space for clear thinking that resists the encroaching build-up of communication.

Simply reducing your phone use by 30% might be a good start.

Remember Deresiewicz' 'most excellent sheep'?

Lambs to the slaughter?

I have a sneaky feeling that being unGoogleable is the ultimate in chic. Off grid. Unconnected. Rogue.

Googling yourself and finding zero results.

A 'tech-no'.

Going forward, that has to be the cooooolest thing ever.

Part 7
DARINGLY HAPPY

> **Thought for the day**
>
> Thank goodness they got the design for the drawing board right first time!

First Up, a Story …

Dances? Which ones did you grow up with? Hokey cokey for sure? But after that? YMCA? Macarena? Lambada? You'll have pushed a pineapple and shaken a tree in your time. Have you galloped your way across a dance floor, Gangnam style?

For this next section to work, Will wants you to know that The Floss is a dance. Kids across the land are doing it.

The Floss. It's a fast and furious dance craze. That's all you need to know.

Next door to me lives a young man whom I'm convinced might just prove to be the saviour of humanity. He may be three years old, but I most certainly wouldn't describe him as 'only', three years old. Teddy, you see, is a lesson to us all. He's not learnt differently, see. He's too cool to be too-cool-for-school. When it comes to life, he's the physical embodiment of the ghost of Christmas past, present and that which is to come – and not just at Christmas. Teddy jingles exceedingly well all year around. I'll give you just one such example of little Ted's brilliantly impulsive take on life.

Whilst I was wandering down the garden path the other day, Ted's mum popped her head out of the upstairs window to mention something relatively innocuous; one of those neighbourly insights that's useful to know but not particularly earth-shattering in magnitude. It probably had something to do with a wheelie bin. The conversation was rapidly hijacked by young Ted, who simply couldn't contain himself; he was fit to burst and somehow individually a whole lot greater than the sum of his constituent parts. Which is no mean feat. He was desperately excited, and desperate to share his enthusiasm. I was desperate to hear it. Looking at Ted's effervescence, I needed a bit of whatever he had.

After wrangling his way to the front of the window and being harnessed by the scruff of the neck by his slightly apprehensive-looking mother, Teddy made his proclamation. At full volume. He was looking at me, but I could sense that he was addressing the world at large. 'Will … Will! Look! Dental floss! I'VE GOT DENTAL FLOSS!!!' Ted was brandishing an invisible thread of hope in the universal battle against tooth decay. Just to make sure the message had been received, Ted vociferously repeated the statement, with no negligible loss of amplitude. I smiled awkwardly, being slightly unsure of what the correct response should be. I thought too hard about it, when what I should really have done was to, well – floss. The dance. Fast and furious. Right there and then, I should have dropped everything and flossed.

His invisible thread for my whole-body phantasmagorical floss would've no doubt sent both Teddy (and his mum) into raptures of stratospheric proportions.

But I didn't, and I so wish that I had. The moment had passed. It's a regret, a missed opportunity.

But also a learning opportunity.

Smiling weakly, stepping to the back of the queue and suppressing your urge to floss? As a rule, it's surely better to realize that you can do something, rather than you could've done something. Life: you've got to be receptive, open and up for it. After all, what's the best that could happen?

Welcome to the weird and wonderful world of being daringly happy. Here are some top tips that might require some courage.

Fortune favours the brave.

Happiness leakage. We dare you!

Bottom Fever

> ### Mbuki-mvuki. Swahili
>
> To take off in flight (mbuki), to dance wildly (mvuki). Literally, to shed clothes in order to dance; possible origins of the phrase 'boogie woogie'.

It is possible to get excited and be exciting. *Again.*

You can smile and laugh and beam and craft and create and relish. If you allow it. If you disavow the shackles of artificial adulthood and just react rather than overthink how you should be reacting.

Of course, it's quite hard to 'just be you' rather than continually doing what you think is expected of you.

Be the sort of mother, father, brother, sister, aunt, uncle, grandma, grandad, best friend, next-door neighbour your child wants you to be. That you want you to be. That you owe it to yourself to be. That deep down you are, and always have been, but have somehow been left stranded on a deserted railway platform with a red-spotted handkerchief.

It's time that the real you made a comeback and proved that you've never really been away.

With that in mind, here's a dancing dare. Apparently, if you use your backside to draw the letters of your name in mid-air, you get *Saturday Night Fever*. Yes, you become an actual John Travolta.

Try it. You might need a friend to record it. Stick it online and then relax with a drink and slice of cake. In a year's time, you will feel all fuzzy and warm when FaceTube reminds you that it happened one year ago today.

That's what we call 'using social media for exactly the right reasons'. Cool, eh?

There's probably a significant proportion of you who are now hesitating; grappling with grown-up internal dialogue contemplating the merits of attempting Saturday-Night-Bottom-Fever.

You're seeking your own permission.

Be John Travolta. Be Olivia Newtron Bomb. Dancing Queen.

You're overthinking it. Remember from the previous section, it's like NOT flossing at Ted.

Social Deviance

James Dean was a rebel with cool hair but no cause. Here's a rebel you've never heard about, a mysterious artist from Bury who goes by the name of Wanksy.

Stick with it folks.

> 'Without deviation from the norm, progress is not possible.'
>
> *Frank Zappa (whose child is called 'Moon Unit' by the way. True)*

He's kind of like Banksy, in that nobody actually knows who he is, but rather than daub on walls, Wanksy finds potholes and draws penises around them. I've assumed Wanksy's male because it's such a blokey thing to do.

His purpose is one of moral good. By turning potholes into dicks it forces the council to come out and sort the pothole p.d.q. It's local activism of the comedic kind.

We're falling short of daring you to break the law but if you're going to be a warrior for social justice, we encourage you to do it with humour.

Laldy Mondays

Gav is a trainer. And he also does comedy. So here are two thoughts …

First, have you ever watched improvised comedy? It's even more terrifying than stand-up because you're thrust on stage with no rehearsal, no script and no clue as to what's about to happen. A situation unfolds and your job is to make something of it, preferably something entertaining.

Improv. You react. You make something up. You think on your feet. I can't help thinking it's exactly like actual real life.

Second, I've been performing and speaking publicly since I was 18 years old. Comedy has taken me all over the world and yet I've never had any formal training, was never a member of a drama club and am definitely not a theatre luvvy. But I am gifted with the ability to turn up, take to the stage and – in true Scots dialect – *'gie it laldy'* (translation: give it all you can, and more).

I live my life by what I refer to as the 'Opening Night Principle'. What does this even mean?

In the world of the performing arts, cast and crew await Opening Night with an abundance of hope, anticipation, excitement and terror. This is it, everything they've worked towards, it's what it's all about. It's their first night with an actual audience. Get this right and we're off and running with 5-star reviews, full houses and standing ovations. People – cast, crew, audience – they all leave buzzing, energized, moved. We all want more, it feels sensational for all involved. Roll on the second night.

Now apply this to daily life. Work, school, study, relationships, health, fitness, family. What if we made the effort to not just get up each day but to truly turn up and treat the day as if it were your opening night?

'Don't be careful. You could hurt yourself.'
Byron Katie

My first 'proper job' was primary school teaching – 26 kids in a room from 9 a.m. until 3:30 p.m. The best teachers are the ones who turn up and *gie it laldy.* Just as are the best leaders, the best parents, friends, lovers, etc.

The Opening Night Principle is an energy that makes people tick, lifts a room and can have huge impact on all those around. It has a natural excitement to it but it also brings an edge. The thrill of possibilities, a touch of the unknown. Adding an extra dollop of passion to your emotional soup.

Hell yeah. Improv your way through life, and *gie it laldy.*

Especially on a Monday!

Be Loud and Proud

Previously, we encouraged you to announce your plot twists. This time we'd like to up the ante and announce when you're having a happy moment. You can celebrate it however you want, from a *Harry Met Sally* orgazmatron to punching of the air or a heel-clicking dance around the grocery aisle.

Notice your moments and announce them to the world. *'I'm having a happiness moment ...'*

'I'm having a happiness moment! Whoop!'

Dare to be a little bit odd. Become known as the family member who announces their happiness moments! Because calling them out rubs off on everyone.

Or save them up for the dinner table. It's the perfect place to gather and re-live them. You smile more. Your children smile more. Your adults smile more. You rediscover an appetite for life.

Happiness, like depression, is a self-reinforcing cycle. It's an upward spiral. Happiness enhances volition, which in turn increases happiness, and away you go. Indeed, the greatest gift of happiness may not be in the feeling itself but rather in the accompanying thrill of possibility. Suddenly the world is in full surround sound HD 3D Technicolor! The eye sees more clearly, the mind thinks more keenly, the heart beats faster and everything seems possible.

So we're advocating that you announce your happiness moments. Share them. And encourage others to do the same.

A Quiet Thank You to the Carers

Purpose sounds big – ending world hunger or eliminating nuclear weapons – they're BIG.

But it doesn't have to be. You can also find purpose in being a good parent to your children, creating a more cheerful environment at your office or making a giraffe's life more pleasant.

Story time. Another true one.

'The next thing I remember,' Erik said, 'was driving in the car out to Stony Brook Hospital and not knowing how serious it was, what condition she was in, where she was hit, or if she was alive.'

He eventually learned that his little girl was in surgery with a paediatric neurosurgeon.

That gave Erik three pieces of information. Number one: his daughter was alive. Number two: this was serious. Number three: *neurosurgeon*, she had a brain injury.

At the hospital, Erik was led to a private waiting area, where the brain surgeon came in to see him and his wife. The surgeon explained that Katy was in a medically induced coma. Her vitals were stable but the doctor explained that they'd had to relieve the pressure on her brain by removing a piece of skull.

Erik and his wife were numb. They drank rubbish coffee from a machine and stayed by their daughter's bedside. Late that night, her intracranial pressure spiked and she was wheeled into theatre once more.

Erik held his wife. 'Where is the good in any of this?'

When Kate came out of her second brain surgery the doctors transferred her to Mount Sinai Hospital in New York City, where she underwent intensive rounds of therapy. Because of the accident, she could no longer speak, her depth perception was impaired and she had lost nearly all of her memories.

Miraculously, by October, Katy was able to return to school part-time and continued to attend rehab. Everything was super-slow. Remember, she was missing a chunk of skull.

By November, the little girl was well enough to return to Stony Brook so that the doctors could replace the missing jigsaw piece of bone. This would be her third brain surgery or as her dad describes, 'It was kind of a triumphal re-entry.'

It seemed that, despite the odds, Katy was going to make it. Erik continued searching for the meaning in everything that had happened: *I'm grateful she's alive*, he admitted on the eve of her third brain surgery, *but I don't know how much more of her I am going to get back*.

Again, he returned to the question: *Where is the good in any of this?*

He found it when Katy came out of the surgery. The two of them were in the recovery room. His daughter was still woozy from the anaesthesia when a series of visitors began arriving at her bedside.

The first person to come was a doctor. 'Katy, you wouldn't remember me,' she said. 'I'm the admitting physician who was in the emergency room the day you came in.'

Moments later, a smiling nurse popped by: 'Hi Katy, great to see you on the mend. You won't remember me, but I was the nurse who was there when the original operating team came and started working on you.'

'Katy, you wouldn't remember me,' another guest said, 'but I was the chaplain on duty when you came in and I spent time with your parents.'

The grapes were piling up!

'Hi Katy,' said the next person, 'you won't have a clue who I am, but I was the social worker who liaised with school.'

'And I was the nurse on your second surgery,' said another beaming visitor.

According to her dad it was 'a parade of smiling faces'.

The last visitor was a nurse named Nancy Strong, who had overseen Katy's stay in the intensive care unit over the summer. Erik pulled her aside and said, 'You know, I think it's great that you are all coming by to wish Katy luck. But there's something else going on here, isn't there?'

'Yeah,' Nancy said, 'there is. For every ten kids we see with this injury, nine of them die. There is only one Katy. We need to come back and we need to see her, because she is what keeps us coming back to work in this place every day.'

And Erik realized, *this is the good.*

Teachers, nurses, cleaners, therapists, physiotherapists, radiologists, doctors, teaching assistants, doctors' receptionists, road sweepers, charity workers, dinner ladies, dinner men, bin men, bin ladies, paramedics, navy/army/airforce, traffic wardens, post office workers, police, surgeons, people who shine the floors in schools using those whirly polishing things, librarians, carers; thank you.

Thank you for caring.

There's something called 'compassion fatigue'. Teachers, for example, have a remit to educate youngsters. The likelihood is that you will be paid commensurate with your skills and qualifications but the emotional labour of the job doesn't feature in the job description. It's emotionally draining because you care.

Thank you for caring.

Your bin collection team will be paid a bin collection wage that takes no account of the fact that there's a whole shebang of emotional detritus that comes with the bin bag detritus.

Bin men, bin women, bin children, *thank you for caring.*

Paramedics, you are paid a paramedic amount of money that reflects your qualifications and training. You're not paid extra for engaging with the old lady whose husband has just passed away, yet you do it anyway. That extra five minutes really matters. Human connection.

Thank you for caring.

Shortly before he died of cancer Kenneth Schwartz wrote, *'Quiet acts of humanity have felt more healing than the high-dose radiation and chemotherapy that hold the hope of cure. While I do not believe that hope and comfort alone can overcome cancer, it certainly made a huge difference to me.'*

Anyone in a caring profession, whatever your job and whatever pay grade you're on, or indeed whether you're caring for an elderly relative for no pay whatsoever, I thank you for your 'quiet acts of humanity'.

Thank you for caring.

Pass it on.

Give Out 'I Love You' Hugs

Social touch is being nudged from our lives. In the UK, doctors have been warned to avoid comforting patients with hugs lest they provoke legal action, and a government report found that foster carers were frightened to hug children in their care for the same reason. We three authors often work in schools and, quite frankly, it can be awkward when kids hug you. Instinctively, we want to hug back. But should we? Are we allowed to?

In the UK, half a million older people go at least five days a week without seeing or touching a soul. That's the saddest sentence in the entire book.

Modern society has demonized touch to a level at which it sparks off hysterical responses and legislative processes. Of course, this lack of touch is not good for mental health.

Touch is commonly thought of as a single sense, but it is much more complex than that. Some nerve endings recognize itch, others vibration, pain, pressure and texture. And one exists solely to recognize a gentle stroking touch.

If you're unconvinced, Google 'Harry Harlow' and read about his famous monkey experiments. Here's the headline news: unloved baby monkeys retreat to a corner, self-harm and stare into space. Mary Carlson (worked alongside Harlow) describes touch as 'a sort of species recognition'.

Which suggests that without touch, humans may be, well, less human.

Tiffany Field (academic, working in Miami) weighs in by saying what we're all noticing, 'You just don't see people touching each other these days.' She has just come from a restaurant, 'And everybody was on their cell phones.' At LaGuardia airport recently, she walked around the waiting area. 'Not a soul was touching another. Even two-year-olds were sitting in carriages with iPads on their laps.'

So our happiness dare is to touch. Not 'grope', 'mither' or 'harass'. There will be a dozen people in your life who are emotionally close enough to hug, so treat them to a 7-second embrace. Don't count out loud. In fact, don't say a word. Just hold them close for a full 7 seconds.

It's an 'I love you' hug.

Drop Dead Happy

Here's an interesting way to up your levels of likeability – don't be afraid to be a bit of an idiot. There's something called the 'pratfall effect' (honestly, there really is) whereby scientists have proved that you're more attractive if you celebrate your mistakes.

> 'And those who were seen dancing were thought to be insane by those who could not hear the music.'
>
> *Friedrich Nietzsche*

Imagine the party's slacking, so Will decides to take the bull by the horns and be the first one on the dance floor. Nobody follows. The pratfall effect says that rather than retire sheepishly to the bar he should give it the full Floss. No half measures. Floss for the full 4 minutes.

Revelling in his faux pas and coming off the dance floor with a huge sweaty grin – that ladies and gents, is the key to gorgeousness.

Special Brew and Special Pants

Here's a Scandi happiness hack – the Finnish path to happiness – kalsarikänni (aka 'pantsdrunk').

Pantsdrunk is simple. The clue is in the title. And hats off to the Finnish government for having enough national deprecation to have endorsed the concept by introducing two emojis of people drinking in their underwear in armchairs – a man in briefs with a beer and a woman with a glass of red wine – to represent Finnish culture.

'Pantsdrunk' is exactly as it sounds. This route to happiness literally means 'drinking at home, alone, in your underwear'.

Oh, those cheeky Finns, they've opted for something that's the antithesis of posing and pretence. It's a single finger salute across the Baltic to the Danes and their super sexy 'hygge'. One does not post atmospheric images on Instagram whilst pantsdrunk. 'Here's me relaxing at home, in string vest and Y-fronts, enjoying a Carling 6-pack – on my own.' It's not you at your best. Or, if it is, God help you.

> 'If you ever start taking things too seriously, just remember that we are talking monkeys on an organic spaceship flying through the universe.'
>
> *Joe Rogan*

We like pantsdrunk because it has a twinkle in its eye. It's about being real. It's about letting go. There's zero performance. I would imagine it's quite liberating to get home from work, peel your kit off and reach for a tinny. I think the British version would need some pork scratchings?

Delving a bit deeper, it seems pantsdrunk doesn't need to be a solo activity. According to *The Guardian* 'It can also be enjoyed with a good friend, housemate, or perhaps a relative … when practised properly, pantsdrunk with one's spouse or significant other expands and deepens the relationship.'

So, there you have it. Next Valentine's night, forget the expensive night out and treat your loved one to a relaxed night in. Sitting around half naked with your wife and mother-in-law, who knows what might happen.

A few points of pantsdrunk clarity. It is not about getting wasted. Make sure you only drink according to your needs and abilities.

If we look beyond the humour, pantsdrunk is one more way to celebrate the importance of relaxation. It's an attitude and philosophy that starts from inner peace. It's not really about alcohol at all, it's about taking time out, indulging in a little of what you enjoy and being authentic.

Best of all, pantsdrunk does not require expensive furniture, artisanal hot chocolate, scented candles and a gluten-free cushion – just your drink of choice, closed curtains, a comfy sofa and a TV show you're happy to binge watch.

Lots of lifestyle trends tell you to switch off your phone and get outside. Wouldn't you rather be inside with a bottle of brown ale, working your way through a series on Netflix?

Semi naked?

Of course, if you *did* want to post some pictures, let's follow each other!

#ZESTPantsDrunk

Now that's a happiness dare!

Part 8
COMPOUND INTEREST

Be the Milk

Gav first.

I've always thought that school, work and life in general are very much like a big bowl of Rice Krispies. (Other puffed rice cereals are available, but inferior.)

Bear with me on this one …

Imagine you pour your Rice Krispies into the bowl. Just the Rice Krispies, nothing else.

How would you describe them? Remember there's only Rice Krispies in the bowl, don't get ahead of yourself people.

Literally, just plain Rice Krispies, nothing else, describe them.

I'm pretty sure you'll be thinking about words such as 'dry', 'quiet', 'boring', 'bland' and my favourite, 'beige'.

There is nothing exciting about a bowl of Rice Krispies.

But then you add the milk.

What happens?

Exactly! They SNAP, they CRACKLE and they POP.

They FIZZ, they BANG and they WHIZZ.

You can see them moving before your very eyes. They come alive!

But what happens if you don't get stuck in, devour them, top them up, sprinkle sugar on or refresh them?

They turn to mush. They become 'meh'.

Like work and life. And family even.

If we don't get stuck in, devour them, pay attention to them and give them everything, then guess what? They turn to mush. They become 'meh'. They cease to snap, crackle and pop.

So if work and life are the Rice Krispies, then that must make *you* the milk.

So with a sentence never used in a book ever before, my message to you is simple.

Dear readers … *be the milk!*

Will, Andy, over to you …

Added Interest

Be the milk. Be the vital ingredient that makes everything snap, crackle and pop.

How?

We've deviated a long way from God's original plan, which was for us to hang out in a garden with some naked vegetarians. And while human beings aren't the fastest, biggest or strongest animals on earth, and we don't have the best sense of smell or eyesight, we dominate the planet.

How is it that humans have built cities and empires, and crocodiles remain as dinosaurs? Why do yaks still do what yaks have always done? Why do mules not write poetry? (Hooves, probably. I'm guessing it's hard to bash out a manuscript.) Or, less ridiculously, our nearest relatives, apes – why have they not managed to get a rocket into the cosmos or a monkey on the moon? Or at least learned to boil a kettle?

Here's why.

Go back half a million years and our ancestors – Neanderthals – were eking out a living on our hostile planet. Then (and nobody quite knows how) a new type of human was bred, Homo sapiens ('wise man'), with an upgraded brain that required a new skull shape. Neanderthals had skulls which were backwards heavy. Their brains had a large rear part which was (and ours still is) about motor skills. I would imagine that they were good at running, jumping, throwing and balancing, but not much else.

The new-fangled sapiens developed a neocortex, the bit above your eyebrows where the creases are forged. And BOOM! this gave us the ability to think, to reflect on the past and to imagine the future. Whereas we'd always been very good at responding to the immediacy of emotions ('Sabre tooth tiger! FUCKING RUN!') the neocortex gave us the ability to rationalize and empathize.

We remain the only species on the planet who has the ability to imagine things that aren't here.

Hence, Homo sapiens' brain development accelerated away. The Neanderthals couldn't keep up. They were the modern-day equivalent of red squirrels. The Homo sapiens were the greys: quicker, smarter and better foragers. As with squirrels, they dominated. The red squirrels and Neanderthals – they're toast.

Cut to today and the human brain continues to evolve. It's a super sophisticated anticipating machine. Probabilities, predictions, scenarios, likelihoods, memories, emotions, other people's emotions – your brain scans the near future and chooses a course of action for you. It computes all this in a milli-second, often without you being aware that there's a mass of data being sifted.

Your brain requires a lot of fuel (it's 2% of your body weight but uses 20% of your body's energy) so evolution has designed us to conserve neural energy. The more familiar something is the less energy we spend on it, hence for efficiency purposes, habits of thinking get grooved in.

Your big routines have a series of subroutines looping within them, so not only do you learn to put your socks on before your shoes (otherwise it's socially awkward) but you also have a habit of putting a certain sock on first. Always. But before you put your socks on, you had chosen some underwear (no sane person puts their socks on before their pants), and from 23 pairs of knickers you chose the ones you're currently wearing. Why? Because your brain calculated a mass of scenarios, so your knickers will have been chosen according to the kind of day your brain is anticipating. If it's Saturday night you might be wearing your special ones, in hope. But if you're about to go and do some gardening you've got your rubbish pants on. Your brain has sorted it, on autopilot, knowing that if you wear your special pants for gardening there'll be some chafing, and if you wear your gardening pants on Saturday night someone's going to be disappointed.

This is all going on algorithmically, under the bonnet (so to speak). The neocortex has enabled us to dominate the planet, but my goodness it's got a lot to answer for. The very thing that has allowed us to take over the world has, all of a sudden, turned against us.

Thinking is great. Imagination is amazing. But *over*thinking and *over*imagining? Ruminating, worrying, stressing about the past and panicking about the future – all the things a yak can't do – that's what's killing us.

Enter a 6-syllable word. Now, most 6-syllable words are rock hard. Saponification? You've no idea. Plasmodesmata? Ditto. Antepenultimate? Is that even a word?

But stick 'neuro' and 'plasticity' together and it kind of makes sense. The 'neuro' bit is easy. That's your brain. And 'plasticity' is flexible, bendy, like Plasticine or Play-Doh.

Your brain has neuroplasticity. It's a shape-shifter, adapting and changing according to experience. You can shape it.

So think of this next section as a rewiring exercise. It's about creating habits. *Good* ones. But before we let you loose with the job of rewiring, we need to make sure you're qualified.

We don't want any nasty shocks.

Before you grab the pliers and have a go, you need to know about habits. Three things. I'd say this is the most important part of the entire book, so sit up, take a couple of deep breaths …

And away we go

First up – what does practice make?

No. Not 'perfect'. That's a fib. If you're practising to be perfect, you'll die practising.

In positive psychology, practice makes *permanent*. Indeed, there's a saying that neurons that fire together wire together. Basically, the 2%ers from Andy's research (those who are stand-out happy) have shaped their brains to be more positive.

Individuals who inhabit the upper end of their happiness spectrum have a set of *keystone* habits; habits that, once adopted, will reverberate into other areas of your life, which makes acquiring other desirable habits more natural and requiring of less effort.

These keystone habits provide exponential breakthroughs.

A habit like 'joining a running club' has exponential properties. It'll make you fit, give you more energy, increase your focus and mental performance, raise your metabolism, create proper friendships and so on. Its benefits reverberate out across other areas of your life, making many other positive habits and skills easier to acquire.

The second important point about habits is that small habits are like compound interest. They add up. For example, on Monday, instead of a burger you choose a salad. On that day, there is no difference. You won't notice in the mirror. You won't even notice by Friday. But in two years' time, or ten years down the line, the habit of salad after salad after salad will have made a compound difference. You'll be able to see the result in the mirror.

And what's the point of going to your French night class on a rainy Tuesday. You're not actually going to learn French in an hour anyway. There will be almost no difference. But in 52 weeks it will have made a huge difference. Going to France and being fluent in French, that's a noticeable change.

Ditto, having an extra half an hour in bed and skipping the gym. What difference is today going to make? In line with the other examples, very little. *Today!* But a habit, grooved in, becomes 'the way you are'.

As for your book, the one you've been meaning to write. What difference will today make? It's Saturday so I'm gonna chill. I'm not exactly going to finish the thing by 5 p.m. today. True. But Saturday after Saturday after Saturday …

The healthy food, weekly French lessons, regular gym attendance and dedicated writing are examples of compounding habits that, over time, will change your life.

Fit, healthy, bilingual, and with manuscript written and ready to be sent off to the publisher – that's a really good use of your next 52 weeks.

It's easy (and rather painful) to work them the other way. Daily burgers, no French, wasted gym membership and 52 Saturdays free from writing? They're the easy options, but they'll compound too. You'll be able to look in the mirror in 12 months and see the difference compounding on your waistline, your lethargy, your book is still not started *et still non speak-e de Frenchy.*

Thirdly, not all habits are equal. Some keystone habits provide higher rates of return because they provide benefits that then make adopting subsequent habits easier. Therefore, it makes sense to use your energy to develop habits with the highest rate of return first, and then move on to other desired habits later.

The following section is a mishmash of habits gleaned from Dr Andy's own research, alongside those that shine out from the literature, plus some gleaned from the science of the bleedin' obvious.

We're about to outline seven keystone, compounding habits. These seven are exponential. They turn you into the milk. They will have a positive impact in all the other aspects of your life. Get them embedded in your life and there will be a lot of snap, crackle and popping.

These habits are going to seem ridiculously simple. Because they are.

But sticking at them until they become grooved in? That ain't so easy!

Remember, if you leave the milk on too long, the cereal becomes silent and soggy. So new milk, every day!

Here come some full fat solutions.

1. Cultivate Optimism and Hope

My own research points to one particular keystone habit that scales more exponentially than others. Let's hear a drum roll for the habit that gives you the best psychological bang for your buck … the habit that makes other habits easier to acquire …

Choosing to be positive.

Yeah. I know! After 12 years of hard work, that's the best I can come up with. It's my most significant finding.

Two things; I suspect it's not quite as obvious as it sounds and it's definitely a whole lot more powerful than it sounds.

Let's take a simple example. A lot of people don't particularly want to go to work. If there was a choice to be had, they'd rather give it a miss. You go to work because you need the money. Mortgage payments, gas bills, mouths to feed, car to run … I *have* to go to work.

My research points to something fundamental. It dares to ask the question, 'Now I'm here, how do I make the most of it?' It's less about what you're doing and much more about who you're being while you're doing it.

That's where attitude kicks in.

The point sounds simple enough, but the question is how? *How do I choose to be positive?*

Emotions work in a loop with your thinking. Basically, everything kicks off with a thought.

And here's where optimism and hope get their big break. I'd suggest that these are two vastly undervalued thoughts. Indeed, without optimism and hope, our ancestors might never have ventured far from their tribes and we might all be cave dwellers, still huddled together and dreaming of light and heat. They are ways of thinking that manifest in optimistic and hopeful feelings. Optimism and hope are emotions that yaks don't feel.

Crucial in all of this is that your current mood affects your thinking in three important ways.

Firstly, when you're in an upbeat mood, you think fast and effortlessly. You are more creative and willing to take a bit of a risk so optimism means you have a tendency to give things a go. The opposite is true when you are in a negative mood. You can become fixated on the problem, ruminating and worrying so hard that a solution is hard to come by. Thinking is slow, ponderous and circuitous. Your default answer is a sure-fire 'can't do'. No hope leads to a state of learned helplessness, aka, giving up. You can quit on getting out of bed, your dreams and even life itself.

Secondly, mood also affects what you remember. If you're in a good mood and someone asks you about life you're more likely to colour things positively and, once again, the opposite is true if you're in a pessimistic mindset. Most profoundly, if you stick points 1 and 2 together, your present mood affects your decision making and therefore your future. Optimistic thoughts mean that your future looks bright and your ambitious goals seem achievable, so you are spurred on to do your best to get there. And when you're in a negative or 'cold' state, you view the future through your current bleakness and nothing looks worthwhile.

Positive psychology's brand of optimism is not about being positive all the time but about entertaining the possibility that things could work out. Earlier, we called it 'realistic optimism'. In this respect, the benefit of optimism comes from being open to it, not from blindly following it even when it makes no sense to do so.

Essentially, it's a shift towards asking yourself 'what's the best that might happen?' That simple question opens up a line of options that worrying closes down.

2. Shake Your Ass

Exercise. Not something I looked at in my research, but something I really wish I had. Everyone knows the benefits of regular exercise (makes you look super sexy, prevents obesity, reduces the risk of heart disease, stroke and a smattering of various types of cancer. It also improves your mood, gives you more energy, improves the quality of your sleep, your sex life, and some evidence indicates it even improves concentration and learning).

Edgar Allan Poe summed it up better than we three can with *'The best things in life make you sweaty.'*

Look, I'm not an expert on exercise. I'm not going to attempt to list the do's and don'ts because the short answer is DO.

SOMETHING.

ANYTHING!

MOVE. EVERY DAY.

Here endeth my knowledge on the subject.

It's beyond obvious. Prioritize exercise. Make it part of your day. It's a keystone habit, so everything else in your life will improve (except maybe your knees).

#JFDI

3. Invest in Relationships

I think many of us, if we slow down long enough to take a look at ourselves, don't give our relationships the time or attention necessary to keep them healthy and happy.

You see, it turns out loneliness has become a really big thing. It's growing at an alarming rate, particularly among older people. Various academic papers point to loneliness being just as bad for your physical health as obesity or heavy smoking.

It also makes you miserable and far more susceptible to depression. So paradoxically, in our 'hyper-connected' world, more and more people are finding it harder to take the time to simply be with somebody else for a while. An actual real person.

Here's a challenging activity. I want you to write down the top 10 happiest *moments* of your life. Think hard now.

1

2

3

4

5

6

7

> 8
>
> 9
>
> 10

Your list will be like my list – an eclectic mix of experiences, with two things in common; all done with people you love and none involving Wi-Fi.

The other notable thing is that these happiness experiences are subjective, as in, it's different for different people.

Happiness and relationships are like chicken and egg. It doesn't matter which comes first. They're related.

To bastardize Bananarama, it ain't what you do, *it's the people you do it with.* That's what gets results. So re-read our technology chapter, toss your phone into a lake and invest in real people.

4. Strip Down

We all want to be happier. It's the number one thing from across cultures that people want for themselves and, more so, their kids. So how about this for a philosophical ponderance, a question I often ask when delivering my workshops in schools:

I've invented a happy pill. If you take it, you'll never have to feel sadness ever again. Just one yummy pill, and the effect is guaranteed to last forevs.

Would you take the pill?

The answer, almost unanimously, is no.

How bizarre?

But then again, not so weird. This philosophical conundrum takes us underneath the skin of happiness, towards meaning.

'Many creative people are finding that creativity doesn't grow in abundance, it grows from scarcity – the more Lego bricks you have doesn't mean you're going to be more creative; you can be very creative with very few Lego bricks.'

Jorgen Vig Knudstorp

Personal development comes in flavours. Of the month.

At the time of writing, it's passion and purpose. We like these flavours because we've been writing about them for a good ten years, way before they became a la carte.

The common complaint seems to be from people who have failed to ignite their passion, or failed to find their purpose.

There's a small possibility that this might be true. But there's a much bigger possibility that you've found your passion but are just ignoring it. And that you have a purpose, just not the right one.

Seriously, you're awake for 16 hours a day, what the heck do you do with your time? You're doing *something*, obviously. You're talking about *something*. There's some topic or activity or idea that dominates a significant amount of your time.

Here's how it is. When you move into a house, an *old* new house, it might look a bit run down but you can see that it has potential. There are quick wins, like curtains, carpets, new lamps – and there are bigger jobs, like a new kitchen, fireplace, snazzy furniture.

The horrible job is decorating. I'm talking an old house, remember? And the very worst part of decorating is getting the old paper off the walls. If you've ever had to do it, I promise you, it's proper hard work. Sometimes there are layers and layers of old wallpaper where people have papered over the previous drab paper with something equally drab.

The problem with your passion and purpose is that you might have accidentally papered over them.

This activity might help peel back a layer or two …

Activity: Passion Finder

What do others say you're good at?

What are you good at?

What do others say is your passion?

What is your passion?

What do people turn to you for?

What do you stand for?

Have you ever exceeded your own expectations? In what way?

If those questions are too tricky, here's a super-cool question – indeed, it might be the ONLY question you need to ask to uncover your purpose and passion. It removes all the old layers of paper in nine glorious words:

What makes you forget to eat, poop and sleep?

5. Counting Sheep

Sleep? A compounding habit? Really?

Yes, really.

And you three authors are sleep experts, are you?

[Cue us looking sheepish and avoiding eye contact.] We're non-experts, hence, this is a very brief section. If you Google 'sleep hygiene' you'll get all sorts of wonderful sleep tips that fall into the category of *'I already bloody well knew that!'*

Sleep is such an obvious good habit, rather like choosing to be positive, it is *so* simple that it often gets overlooked. In fact the hurly burly of modern life means we haven't got enough hours in the day so sleep gets squeezed out. We get by on less kip.

Stop skipping your kipping!

Don't imagine that having a lie in on Sunday negates all the sleep you skipped Monday to Saturday. Don't get by on 5 hours. Most people need 8.

A University of Warwick study suggests that good sleep is worth about £200k of mental wealth.

So treat yourself to a lottery win and grab a regular 8 hours.

Sleep-eezy

If you can't sleep, instead of counting sheep, count what you're grateful for starting at A and going through to Z. Just one rule, if you get to X (which you most probably won't), you're not allowed to be grateful for Xylophones or X-rays. They're too easy.

6. Your Daily Daley

In the 1980s, Britain had one of the all-time athletic greats: the moustachioed and supremely talented Mr Daley Thomson, now *Sir* Daley, who would routinely whistle his way through the national anthem as he banked another gold medal.

His event was 'events': running, throwing and jumping. Daley was a double-Olympic-winning decathlete.

'Dec' = 10.

He honed his skills and pushed his body to its absolute limits so he could be best of the best in ten disciplines.

Except he didn't.

He trained and trained for *nine* of the ten because, you see, the 1500 metres, that wasn't his thing. He was bloody hopeless at it. Three and a half laps was best suited to tall, skinny, barrel-chested athletes. Daley was chunky. He was exactly the wrong body shape.

Yes, our world-beating super athlete never trained for the 1500 metres. It was the final event of the ten and his aim was to get through it without tripping up.

Oddly, Daley became the best all-round athlete on the planet by absolutely NOT training for one of the events.

The lesson? We all have weaknesses and it's very easy to focus on them. In fact, most businesses spend an inordinate amount of time identifying employee weaknesses and trying to iron them out. Imagine Sir Daley's annual performance review? He'd have sat with his line manager, chatted through his ten disciplines, and they'd have sent him on a course to improve his 1500 metres.

Indeed, Daley might have made some marginal gains in the 1500, but at the expense of serious slippage in the other nine.

Our world beater would have been downgraded to an also-ran.

So work out where your strengths are and play to them. If you haven't a clue what your strengths are (that's more common than you'd imagine) tap 'VIA' into your search engine and take the online test.

As for weaknesses? Do what Daley did. Do just enough so that they don't trip you up.

7. Get Committed to Commitment

The message from *Zest*, butchered to one sentence is something like this: *Start where you are with what you have.* If we stretched to two sentences we might add, *What you have is plenty.* A third might be, *Finding and playing to your strengths is like rocket fuel.*

The remainder of this chapter stretches the book to a fourth sentence along the lines of *It takes effort to be your best self.*

So, picking up from there, let's explore why you should be bothered. The 'e' word – *effort* – is a bit off-putting. Your argument could be why bother to put extra effort over and above what everyone else is doing?

First up, it doesn't matter what everyone else is doing. We're not talking about *their* 4000 weeks and *their* potential, we're talking about *yours.* Therefore, it matters what *you* are doing.

This picture reveals the secret of success. For everyone. Ever.

moment of ~
seemingly ~
Spontaneous
Success ~

CRITICISM

"NOPE"

Crying

'YOU can't
Do that"

Cancelled DATES

Sad
emails   QUITTING
to Mom

JEALOUSY

'NO!   "you're NOT famous
enough To BE famous"

Late NIGHTs   LOSS of
EARLY mornings   FRIENDSHIPS
(Then again, NEW
ones gained)

ReJecTion x
1000 000 000   "Absolutely NOT"

Vulnerable emails
in effort to 'NETWORK'   Sleepless
nights

* Putting yourself out there *

Effort comes in a double whammy of skills and attitude.

It may well take some effort to rethink *how* you think and to inhabit a world of positive mental habits. If you want to be world class at anything, there's a serious amount of effort involved. The current thinking is that 10k hours is what's required to be awesome (another 'fact' that has been whack-a-moled a dozen times). So to become a fabulous cook, a half-decent accountant, a competent writer or a sub-4-hour marathon runner – these things don't happen by accident.

Human flourishing is exactly the same. The first rule of happy club is that you have to be committed to commitment. Training yourself to be a mental ninja of positivity requires effort. In my experience, lots of it! The payback, over your lifetime, is incalculable. The problem is that you might already have spent 10k hours learning to settle into a mediocre bog-standard attitude. 'Making do' or 'getting by' with a default attitude that fits in with everyone else – otherwise known as mediocrity.

Those lazy neurons of negativity have fired together for ten thousand hours. They've wired together. Those pathways through the brain are etched in. They're so easy to follow.

I figure that you can teach people the principles of positive psychology in three hours flat. But you can't, not in a lifetime, teach them to keep *applying* the principles. Fresh milk every day – that's the effort bit.

My PhD respondents haven't bolted positivity onto their lives, they've integrated the principles *into* their lives.

At the core of all human behaviour, most people are seeking more positive experiences and fewer negative experiences. That means an epic life isn't just about generating good feelings. Equally, it's also about being able to put up with bad ones.

Back in the day, the Greek philosophers came up with a complicated word, eudaimonia, which translates as 'the good life'. In a nod to our older readers, yes, it was what Tom and Barbara were attempting and Margot and Jerry were failing at.

To experience a life well-lived you sometimes have to make sacrifices. Not 'killing a goat at full moon' kind of sacrifice, a 'foregoing of immediate happiness' sacrifice. Because, you see, it's very easy to access happiness right here right now. The immediate whoosh of happiness is called hedonism. The modern world has contorted itself to serve every hedonistic need you can think of, and quite a few that haven't even crossed your mind.

Think of hedonism as sex, drugs and rock 'n' roll happiness.

The problem with instant happiness is something called the hedonic treadmill. A glass of wine every night will feel nice and cosy. For a while. Then you need two glasses for the cosy feeling to kick in. Then three.

Then you're screwed.

The hedonic treadmill is like a real treadmill – in the long run you get absolutely nowhere and, if you stay on it too long, it'll kill you.

Remember, practice makes *permanent.* There's effort in creating new habits of thinking and behaving. Unlearning the old and relearning the new ain't easy. That requires a big dollop of something that, in a fast-paced now-now-now society is in short supply; namely, commitment.

To make the point, let's take one of the most painful experiences of Gav's life, the London Marathon. Unbelievable pain, raw nipples, tears at the finishing line. And he didn't even come in the top 10! In fact, he ran his heart out and finished 24,711th.

If Gav wanted instant happiness, he could have stayed in Edinburgh and chomped through a box of Maltesers while watching the whole thing on TV.

Back to that complicated Greek word, eudaimonia. That requires a sacrifice of instant happiness, for long-term life satisfaction. Actually going for a training run and eventually *competing* in the London marathon. That's part of a life well-lived.

Life satisfaction involves choices. Imagine you've rivalled the world old-age record and you're reflecting back over your 127 years. Your major achievements – all the things you're misty-eyed about—they involved pain, effort, struggle, even anger and despair.

Why? Because it's these activities that give you purpose.

Therefore, let us dare pose a question that perhaps you've never considered before. In fact two:

What pain do you want in your life?

What are you willing to struggle for?

Think about it. Could it be that the barriers in life are put there to show how badly you want something? Or, the same point but worked the other way around; if the challenge we face doesn't scare us, then it's probably not that important.

That, dear reader, is a remarkably big thought. So, in the interests of challenging you, it's worth pondering what your big goals might be, and what you're willing to give up to achieve them.

We're asking you for 2 goals, one at work and one outside of work (hobby, sport, music, family?):

Big thing I want to achieve at work

What I'm willing to give up to achieve it

Big thing I want to achieve outside of work

What I'm willing to give up to achieve it

The Greek word euthymia is the sense of our own path and how to stay on it without getting distracted by all the others that intersect it. In other words, it's not about beating or bettering anyone else. It's not about having more than the others. It's about being what you are, and being as good as possible at it, without succumbing to all the things that draw you away from it. It's about going where you set out to go and accomplishing the most that you're capable of in what you choose.

That's euthymia. No more and no less.

Maybe your priority actually is money. Or maybe it's family. Maybe it's influence or change. Maybe it's building an organization that lasts, or serves a purpose. All of these are perfectly fine motivations. But you do need to know.

Moreover, you need to know what you want and what you're willing to endure along the way.

The Shining Path

So, ear plugs at the ready, we're going to get a little shouty. We come full circle, back to rule number 11 of life, GET BOTHERED!

Too often we focus on the darkness, the night sky, stumbling in the shadows instead of radiating light. In reality our pathway comes from within, we're led by what we project.

Some readers will remember *Jamie and the Magic Torch*, a rather lovely flashlight that did more than light up the darkness. Jamie's torch opened up a hole into a fun dimension called Cuckoo Land.

We've all got one of Jamie's Magic Torches. They're called your keystone habits. They will illuminate the way.

Here's a reminder of what we've just thrown at you. Exponential change. It's a whole lot easier when the way forward is lit!

1. Cultivate optimism and hope.
2. Shake your ass. Exercise. Just fucking do it!
3. Invest in relationships.
4. Strip down. Remove the layers. Find your true purpose. If in doubt ask yourself what is it that makes you forget to eat, poop and sleep.
5. Count sheep. Sleep. Treat yourself to a cheeky little lottery win.
6. Be Daley. Daily! Strengthen your strengths and don't let your weaknesses trip you up.
7. Be committed to commitment. A life well-lived requires sacrifices of immediate happiness for long-term satisfaction.

Part 9

MORT TO LIFE

Shape Up

Everyone is able to change. The bigger question is, *are you willing?* It's easy to get stuck in a neurological rut – and become what we call 'hard of thinking'.

> 'Play from your fucking heart!'
> *Bill Hicks*

Our message is simple. Your life is plasticine; it's up to you to shape it. So, no, you can't technically grow younger, but you can in all likelihood become fitter, healthier, happier and more 'you', than you currently are. And you can enjoy doing all the things that you loved doing when you were seven when you're seventy-seven.

Plasticine your life

Aliveness is not just an age thing. You can be wise beyond your years or young at heart or any other combination and more besides. We don't stop doing stuff because we grow old, we grow old because we stop doing stuff.

I've met 25-year olds and 85-year youngs!

As a rule, if you fancy a little change for the better, don't expect life to start dispensing good fortune for free. It may do, but it's a slim possibility. Life is an ATM; the more you deposit, the more there is available to withdraw. There's a much bigger, larger, fatter chance that fortune might be heading elsewhere, in the direction of the risk-takers, who know the unknown is worth embracing and have invested a little effort.

Life? Is there a meaning?

What if Hokey cokey really is what it's all about?

Here's our guide to shaping up. Mentally.

You Are Enough

Let's start bold. If you're gonna be in the room, *be* in the room.

Be present.

Have presence.

'Life sucks, but in a beautiful kind of way.'

Axl Rose

That 'room', of course, being 'life'.

Life's full of cheap seats. Living can feel like a training course, not merely in the sense of continual learning, but because it's tempting to sit at the back. I promise you, often, the entire front row remains empty.

I like the idea of being in the thick of it. The problem with giving life a bloody good go is there's an inevitable risk of failure. Falling over, being mauled, grazed, hurt.

Positive psychology has taught me that life is truly about picking yourself up and cracking on. It's about staying in the game knowing that you're going to get knocked down. Some might call it vulnerability, my definition of which is 'knowing you're going to get kicked in the teeth but being wholehearted about it anyway'.

There will be times (dozens in fact) when life deals you a whole heap of something that stinks to high heaven.

We can't make those times go away. Indeed, in a strange detour from traditional personal development, we ask that you welcome troubled times.

This chapter is less about remedies, strategies or tactics. It's more about it being perfectly okay to stumble and fall. Acknowledge the bruises. Admire them. Learn from them.

And get back on your feet.

Stronger.

I've spent a good chunk of my life fretting about things that didn't need to be fretted about. It seemed to me that everyone else knew what they were doing, as if they'd read the 'guidebook to life' and I'd missed out. How to network, speak in public, make small talk, look confident, walk into a pub on your own, choose the right career path, eat spaghetti in public, chat people up, pronounce quinoa …

Then, at long last, it dawned on me: *nobody gets it.*

There is no manual for life. If at first you don't succeed, guess what, you're normal!

Hoorah!

Nobody actually knows what they're doing. Everyone's making it up as they go along. And the best bit? Everyone is screwed up, broken, clingy and scared. Even the people in your life who seem to have their shit totally together? They actually haven't! They've got the same shrill inner critic as you. The same insecurities and foibles. They actually wonder if their bum looks big. They slump out of bed feeling like they can't do this anymore. They sweat when they have to return something to a shop, even when they have the receipt. They're not sure what the etiquette is for asking for the bill, or what size tip to leave. They have no idea how to pronounce quinoa. As for networking – we all dread it!

Sure, we're all putting effort into *looking* like we know what we're doing. Everyone else puts on a smile instead of showing the inner torment. Everyone else says 'yes' to parties they don't want to go to. Most people are exactly like you – they prefer a quiet night in.

So let's start at first base; congratulations, you are normal.

The modern world will try its damndest to convince you otherwise but take it from us, you are enough.

Embrace Your 'Ordinary Magic'

'The world ain't all sunshine and rainbows. It's a very mean and nasty place, and … it will beat you to your knees and keep you there permanently if you let it. You, me, or nobody is gonna hit as hard as life. But it ain't about how hard you hit. It's about how hard you can get hit, and keep moving forward.'

Rocky Balboa

Therapy and counselling have mushroomed into some sort of 'grief ombudsmen' who you can turn to in troubled times. Happiness is so desirable that if we're not experiencing enough of it, we can get it prescribed.

The mental health system teaches us to be shit-scared of our own thoughts and to keep within the straight and narrow of conventional feelings. We tranquilize, calm and sedate those who go outside of normality. The modern-day notion appears to be edging towards 'there's no need to ever suffer emotionally because you can take a pill for it'. Whatever 'it' happens to be.

Truth time. Pain is inextricably a thread in the fabric of life. To tear it out is not only impossible but destructive because everything else unravels too.

So, let me elucidate on the polar opposite schools of thought as far as 'suffering' goes. The positive version suggests that suffering has a redemptive role to play in life; in all instances there is something to be *gained* from suffering. Admittedly, in the midst of suffering, these learnings aren't always obvious but a traumatic episode can give you a new perspective or an inner strength.

I could give hundreds of examples from my research but I've narrowed it down to one quote from an actual real person. A happy person:

'Since the personal loss of my 11-year-old son, I don't take life for granted since then and try to enjoy every moment of my waking life.'

Come again? Your young son has died and you're still capable of being happy?

It's a powerful example of what academics call 'post-traumatic growth'. Personally, I prefer the term 'ordinary magic', a well of untapped resources that we all have, that enable us to bounce back after a serious setback.

Gosh, it's not easy. And, yes, you're allowed some down time. But the most courageous thing you will ever do is muster the inner resources that you didn't know were there, stare adversity in the face and shove your middle finger back at it.

Fuck you world! I'm coming back stronger!

It's Okay to Be a Sidekick

We're told to think big, live big, to be memorable and dare greatly. We think that success requires a bold vision and undergarments worn on the outside. After all, that's what Branson and Jobs did. Oh, and Mandela and Luther King too. And Bolt and Federer.

But did they? Did they really set out to conquer the world with a sweeping plan?

In 1969, Richard Branson was living in a London commune, surrounded by the British music and drug scene. He came up with the idea to begin a mail-order record company called Virgin to make a few quid. Do you think it crossed his mind to create a juggernaut of a business empire? *I'm gonna sell some magazines so later on I can afford some planes.*

Did Martin Luther King address the crowd at the Lincoln Memorial, waving a detailed step-by-step blueprint of how he was going to bring about civil rights? If his speech had been 'I have a strategic plan and a step-by-step guide …' the people would have trudged home, disillusioned.

'I have a dream …' now that's worth staying for. And buying into.

We see risk-taking swagger and successful people in the media, and, eager for our own successes, try to reverse-engineer the right attitude, strike the right pose.

In a chapter full of controversy, let's chuck a big fat one at you: *it's perfectly okay to play small.*

Gav was delivering one of his legendary workshops in a high school in Scotland. Here's the story …

There were about 100 teenagers in the room. I had asked a question which was swiftly answered correctly by one of the boys, whom I congratulated and asked his name.

'Shaw' he replied.

'Shawn?' I clarified.

Clearly the young man had spent his whole life so far correcting people so with a frustrated tone he corrected my correction; 'SHAW, not Shawn. No "N". Just Shaw.'

'I have never heard that name before, it's cool, I like it. What does it mean?' I asked.

In his broad Scots accent the young man replied, 'Am no tellin ye!'

'Do you actually know what it means?' I asked.

'Aye,' said Shaw.

'So, are you going to tell me?'

'Naw,' said Shaw.

'You have to tell us now! The fact you're not telling me would suggest it has an awesome meaning,' I said.

'Am no tellin ye,' was Shaw's response yet again.

I wasn't for giving up. 'I'll tell you what my name means if you tell me what Shaw means.'

'You go first,' said the lad.

'Gavin means "eye of the hawk" or "hawk of battle". Either way it's like a superhero or a superhero's power.'

Shaw and his pals seemed suitably unimpressed. I piped up again, 'Right, your turn, what does Shaw mean?'

Shaw took a deep breath and sighed. He said nothing.

'C'mon,' I said, 'it canny be that bad. What does Shaw mean? Go for it!'

And with another sigh Shaw finally replied …

'Little row of potatoes.'

The room erupted into a mixture of laughter and clapping.

Another kid commented on the fact 'little row of potatoes' definitely wasn't a superhero name.

I tried my hardest to imagine Marvel launching their latest comic movie, 'Hawk of Battle & the Little-Row-of-Potatoes-Man'. Nothing. My imagination wasn't able. But I decided that if the movie ever did get into production, Little Row of Potatoes would be the sidekick. Like Robin, but a touch more rural.

At the end of the session, as the group were leaving the room, another one of the kids approached me and simply said, 'I've always preferred the sidekicks. In fact I'd rather be a sidekick, they're the real good guys.'

It got me thinking. What if we've got it all wrong? Are we encouraging too many people to be the pants-on-the-outside cape-wearing hero? That's what the movies focus on, but what if we looked again. Sure, the star of the show is the star of the show, but the sidekick is their crutch.

> 'Batman's the triple bacon cheeseburger we paid for. Robin's the garden salad that came with it.'
>
> Wired Cosmos

It's the same with music. Katrina wouldn't have been successful without her Waves. Ian Dury needed The Blockheads as much as The Blockheads needed him. Martha and her Muffins were joined at the hip.

In a sentence that's never been written before, what if some of us are happy being a wave, blockhead or muffin?

In comic book terms, sidekicks open up a narrative and introduce an alternate point of view. S/he brings a more human element to the story, essentially forcing our central character to open up, display their more caring side and share their emotions. The sidekicks also clean up the mess and are happy to step back when the glory is being awarded.

They're loyal and often the reason our hero succeeds. They can also bring much needed comic relief!

What if Tina Turner was right all along and we actually don't need another hero? What if it's okay not to be hogging the limelight? And what if some of us are happier this way?

So it's worth celebrating the sidekicks who are more than happy to *not* be the headline act.

If you're reading this and all you hear from your friends and colleagues is that you should be putting yourself out there more or going for that promotion and yet you really don't want to because you ARE ALREADY DELIRIOUSLY HAPPY. Then good.

'God heard us. He sent help. He sent you.'

Marianne Williamson

Be the best version of you. The you that is happy to *not* be the hero.

Potatoes, you see. They're never the star of the show. But by God do they pull a meal together and warm yer belly.

In another sentence never before written, we're asking you to be the best little row of potatoes you can be.

Embrace Your Inner *Kintsugi*

There's a Latin expression *Materiam superabat opus*: 'the workmanship was better than the material.' Once you've mulled it over you find it's easily applied to life. The material we've been given – genetically, emotionally, financially – that's where we begin. We don't control that. We do control what we do with it. While it may be true that you can't make a silk purse out of a sow's ear, you can craft a great life from not very much.

Here's something bordering on profound. All the way from Japan we bring you *Kintsugi*, the art of restoring pottery.

Except the Japanese don't do it like we do it. When a pot/vase/plate gets smashed they glue it back together with lacquer mixed with powdered gold. So instead of hiding the cracks, *Kintsugi* emphasizes them. In fact it positively celebrates the cracks.

The pot, with all its pieces glued together with goldness, is deemed more beautiful than the original.

Pots are one thing, but can you imagine if we applied the art of *Kintsugi* to people? Or, indeed, to yourself? Celebrating our imperfections as a thing of beauty would be a game changer.

Kintsugi, as a philosophy, treats breakage and repair as part of the history of an object, rather than something to hide.

It's very similar to the easier to pronounce Japanese concept of *wabi-sabi* which Richard Powell describes thus: 'Wabi-sabi nurtures all that is authentic by acknowledging three simple realities: nothing lasts, nothing is finished, and nothing is perfect.'[1]

Go on, say it: *wabi-sabi*.

Quirks, anomalies, uniqueness.

You are *wabi-sabi*. I am *wabi-sabi*. Everyone is *wabi-sabi*. Human beings, beautifully crafted by wear and tear.

Revel in your imperfections. The wobbly boobs, the bullying, being picked last for netball, the mole, your hairy back, the lines on your face; they make you, *you*.

You are flawed beauty.

[1] *Wabi Sabi Simple: Create Beauty, Value Imperfection, Live Deeply.* Richard R Powell. Adams Media Corporation.

Activity: Extracting the Good from the Bad

List 3 significant negative events in your life. What positive message can be taken from these events? (e.g., 'it taught me to be strong', 'it taught me that I can survive')

1)

2)

3)

How can these lessons improve your future?

Forgiveness

In Part 4 we talked about #FakeStress – getting angry about stuff that isn't worth getting angry about. If you want to know more about that particular form of mental self-harm, please read *SHINE*.

This isn't that.

This is a whole lot bigger!

First base, life's plot twists are coming, the whole point being that you don't see a plot twist. It's unexpected. BOOM! Here's a major surprise! Deal with it.

Second base, if you cut out 95% of your low-level grumbling (which is a habit) you'll feel so much lighter. Plus, when you do have a grumble it'll be totally out of character. Because you're not a serious complainer, your occasional complaints carry much more weight.

Third base, we've all been wronged.

Your ego has a massive defence budget. It will be desperate to prove itself right so will argue and hold grudges, sometimes for decades.

Ask yourself, *who exactly are you hurting with that grudge?*

When you forgive you in no way change the past – but you sure do change the future. Inability to forgive means you are holding onto the past – you are punishing yourself. So forgiveness is, first and foremost, for *your* benefit. It means recognizing that you've already been hurt once. You need to give yourself some TLC and let go of this form of mental self-harm.

We're winding ourselves up in our heads, creating the state that we're in. As Zig Ziglar used to say, are you in a right state or THE right state?

There's not some magical thread, like Theseus's ball of string, that connects the present to the past. That shit thing that happened to you way back, that event doesn't exist in the present unless you magic it into life via thinking.

Hey, none of us are perfect!

Gav admits that he used to be the worst for holding grudges. The dickhead in school that was STILL affecting my thinking 10 years later! The years of trying to make it in the world of stand-up, getting so close and it all simply ending overnight. What if? What if? What if?

I've got to step up and learn to take charge of the thoughts that come into my head. I haven't got total control, that'd be like some sort of conscious controlling ninja, but once I'm aware that it's me that's pissing me off (they're my thoughts, I allowed them into my timeline) I can be smarter with the ones that I allow in.

LET IT GO!

We hold onto things and we get angry about injustices because we care. We *really* care.

And we're certainly not advocating that you stop caring.

We're recommending that you care about the *right* things.

Mark Manson has a certain way with words. Maybe he's spot on with 'When we choose to give a fuck about everything, then we feel as though we are perpetually entitled to feel comfortable and happy at all times, that's when life fucks us.'

The problem is priorities. Cutting to the chase, the modern world gives you too many things to get angry about. Don't let stubbornness make a bad situation worse.

Here's the truth.

Moving on, forgiving, getting over things, letting go – these things are not a sign of weakness. They're a sign of tremendous strength.

Plenty of the F-Word

The key to optimism and pessimism lies in our 'explanatory style' – how we explain life events (good and bad) to ourselves.

Here's an example of how explanatory style works. We're going to go gruesome to hammer the point in one go. Let's assume you're waiting at a pedestrian crossing, the little light goes green, the *beep beep* noise signals it's safe to walk so off you go. The drunk driver is too pissed to stop. He hits the accelerator instead of the brake and your body is thrown into the air.

You wake up two days later. Legs in traction. Pelvis shattered. After six months off work and twelve months of rehab, you're back on your feet but will forever have the scars and a bit of a limp.

Looking back on the incident, are you lucky or unlucky?

This hints at your 'explanatory style' and it's more important than it sounds. Those with a *pessimistic* explanatory style will feel like a victim of the drunk driver. It's unfair. All that time off work. All that horrible rehab. Not to mention the stress. It's been the worst 12 months of your life. The limp is debilitating so you need a stick. The injustice will haunt you to your dying day.

An *optimistic* explanatory style means you're still a victim of the drunk driver, but you're more likely to regard yourself as lucky to be alive. Yes, it was unfair, but at least I'm back on my feet and back to work. Thank goodness I've got such an understanding employer and, oh my gosh, isn't the NHS wonderful. All that amazing rehabilitation! For free! It's been a tough year but I'm through it. My life can carry on, albeit with a slight limp.

We've used a graphic example of a shattered pelvis to grab your attention. But your explanatory style pervades every aspect of your life, big and small. Best of all, an optimistic explanatory style is something you can develop.

Here's how.

The 'ABCDE' exercise asks you to keep a journal of events that happen to you, and then you analyse them thus:

'A' is the 'adversity' or event itself. This can be anything from being stuck in traffic, your child being bullied at school or your book proposal being rejected for the tenth time.

'B' is your belief and how you interpret that event. The traffic is always against me, the teachers are rubbish for not protecting my child, my book proposal must be lousy.

'C' is the consequence of that interpretation – your feelings and reactions. Typically, these might be getting angry at the traffic jam, having a rant at the teacher or firing off a terse email to the publisher.

ABC is automatic. It's how most people live their lives. They stop at C and, as a consequence, there's a lot of negativity, anger and middle-finger salutes.

In the journey to healthy optimism you have to experience A, B and C but before you curse, shout or fire the angry email off, get to **'D', which is learning to dispute** your interpretation of the event.

Professor Marty Seligman suggests you do this by providing counter-evidence, or simply asking more questions.

So this might be: I am overreacting? Is a 10-minute traffic jam actually worth me pounding my steering wheel and screaming like a banshee? Is it worth an ulcer?

Or: Is it the teacher's fault? Does the teacher even know about the bullying? Is my child actually being bullied or have they just taken an unfortunate remark a little too personally?

Or: Was my book proposal really so bad? Or is it that there are lots of similar proposals landing on their desk every day, in which case I'll have another go and be a bit more creative.

The book proposal questions take us to **'E', energization**, a positive feeling. Some optimism, which clears the blockages of thinking allowing a way forward to emerge.

Over time, as you get better at disputing your interpretations, it can lead to positive feelings and a rewiring of your mental circuitry. Hence, you can learn to develop an optimistic explanatory style.

The ABCDE exercise is an example of Cognitive Behavioural Therapy, a process of rewiring your neurons in a more positive way.

Here's Gav's real life version of ABCDE. In actual fact, it's much bigger than ABCDE because in the book that keeps on giving, he introduces an F.

> **A = Adversity**. The 20th of March 2012 is still to this day the toughest day of my entire life. This is the day my dad died. He had been battling pancreatic cancer, one of the most aggressive cancers going. It's an utter bastard.
> Fast-forward to Christmas, the first one in my lifetime when my dad wasn't carving the turkey.

B = Belief. It's going to be a tough Christmas without dad. We were sat around the table at mum's house on Christmas Day. Mum, me and my family, my brother and his family, aunts, uncles, cousins and an empty chair. We left the chair for dad, we thought it would be a lovely thing to do. Turns out it was just weird and a tad creepy.

Mum was in the kitchen prepping all the Christmas bits and pieces. She wouldn't let anyone help her, not that we would have anyway, she's an ex PE teacher from Glasgow who smokes cigars (there's an image for you) and in her own words, 'nobody messes with Irene in the kitchen!'

The food was out, the drinks poured but something was missing. Talk. Energy. Happiness.

We all knew why. *Someone* was missing.

C = Consequence. We were all acting like a big bunch of adults. No one was talking about dad for the fear it might upset mum, and no one was celebrating Christmas because it might not be appropriate. Cracker jokes aren't funny at the best of times! We were experiencing a collision of jovial and awkward.

As spuds were spooned and gravy poured, we tucked into our turkey. It was one of those moments where there were lots of knives and forks clanking on plates, but an eerie human silence.

We got it wrong and 4-year-old Kian knew it. Better still, he knew something had to be done.

D = Dispute the thinking. At 4, Kian didn't have many words, just the exact right ones. 'I'm sad as well you know!' exclaimed the wee man. You could feel all the adults in the room stiffen. *Shit! Are we all going to have to share our emotions?*

'You know what Kian, you're absolutely right,' I said. 'We are all sad.'

The knives and forks clanked louder and everyone ate a little faster. Probably nerves?

'I miss my grampa,' he said, shovelling a whole blanketed pig into his mouth. 'It's not the same anymore,' he mumbled through a gobful of pork.

My boy was spot on. You see, my dad *was* Christmas. 'What do you miss most about grampa?' I asked.

Kian swallowed his mouthful and turned to me with a grin. 'Never mind that dad, do you want to see me draw an apple?'

I've no idea where the apple came from but I love a curve-ball. Kids throw them at us all the time. They're like great big beautiful distraction tactics. Everyone around the table burst out laughing. It's what was needed. Something to bring us all back to earth, something silly, something fun, something beautiful. Something wonderful.

E = Energize. I noticed Kian had disappeared. Because that's how you leave the table when you're four, you go down under the table and out. Mum had also left the table. She had opted for the more grown-up traditional leaving method of standing and walking.

All of a sudden she appeared back in the room with a big pile of paper at which point Kian popped back up from under the table with a packet of chunky crayons he'd got that morning from Santa Claus. Mum handed out the paper and Kian gave us all a crayon.

For the next 15 minutes we drew the best apples you've ever seen in your life.

What did I learn in this moment, apart from ABCDE?

Two things.

Firstly, there's an F.

> **F = Fun!** I learned that no matter what you're up against, no matter how hard it gets, draw an apple. Hand out the paper and have an apple drawing competition. Draw the best apples you can and be aware of the great big smile it puts on your face.

Second, I also learned that sometimes you need to allow yourself to step back and see things from a different angle. Reframe. Embrace curveballs. Throw them. Life needs them, they help us to change direction.

Oh, and there's actually a third learning point; next time you leave the dinner table remember … *down, under, out.*

Shine from the Inside Out

I studied bits and bobs of psychology at Uni. Freud was the man with his regaling of the Oedipus Complex (the apparent desire to kill your dad and sleep with your mum), anal character (when your bum becomes charged with energy; who knew?) and good old-fashioned 'penis envy'.

I'll park those gems and bring you 'ego' instead.

Your ego is who you *think* you are.

Your ego's a canny bastard. You can't fight or outsmart it. It's like the fabled 1970s wrestler, Kendo Nagasaki: all you can do is grapple with it and try to unmask it.

To prove that you can be way too clever, we're going to explain 'ego' via Eckhart Tolle (one of the cleverest men in the world), and then Will (a few notches down the cleverness totem pole).

Tolle, the acknowledged guru, first. We all have a sense of 'I'. In normal everyday usage, 'I' embodies an illusory sense of identity that's been referred to as 'an optical illusion of consciousness'.

Your illusory self then becomes the basis for all further thought processes, interactions and relationships. Once you have an identity you can start to hang things on it.

Your ego starts to get heavy. It's like Buckaroo (that bit's not Tolle, that was Will not being able to wait his turn).

You aren't actually the person in the mirror. You're not even the one noticing the person in the mirror. The one who's aware of you being aware. It's the awareness that is prior to the thought. The gap. The formless bit. The bit of you that isn't cells.

Clear?

Of course it's not!

Move over Mr Guru. The riddle of understanding the true nature of self has baffled the finest minds since minds were invented. But hey, Will likes a challenge. Here's his take on the whole shebang.

You are possessed. By your thoughts. You are so totally identified with an incessant stream of involuntary and compulsive thinking and the emotions that accompany it, that you're Regan from *The Exorcist*. If you've never seen the movie, please don't. I watched it in 1979, a pirate copy; it's an 18, I was 8, and am still struggling to un-see it.

Regan was her own worst enemy. She needed exorcizing – no, not sit-ups, squats and burpees – ridding of some bad shit that was inside. I don't want to spoil the plot but it required a priest, there was lots of green spew and it doesn't end well. Especially not for the priest.

Your ego is your identity. You, and your story. You wrote it. You're starring in it. You're directing it. It tells you what your political views are, what you like to watch on TV and who you fancy. It holds onto long-standing resentments, or concepts of yourself as better than or not as good as others, as a success or failure. Your ego is a finely honed comparison machine.

Your sense of self runs through every thought, memory, opinion, emotion, viewpoint and reaction.

Most of us are so fascinated by the content of experience – thoughts, images, feelings, sensations and perceptions – that we overlook the fact that we can stand back and be aware that we're *having* an experience.

If you peek behind the magic ego curtain you'll find this mind hack; cease being fascinated by whatever you are aware of and be interested instead in the *experience of being aware*.

195

Delving deeper into the ego point above, there's a domino effect at work here. The first domino to tip is the realization that 100% of our experience is coming from the inside-out, rather than the outside-in.

Always. In all situations. Forever.

That's one BiiiiiiG domino.

It sure feels like our feelings are coming from the future or past, or shoes, or haircuts. If you've ever had a really bad haircut (a 'scarecut'), you'll know that it ruins your life. Except of course, it doesn't. Domino number 1 says the haircut is neutral. The way you're *thinking* about your bad hair day – that's what's ruining your life.

There's information in your feelings. Your feelings are exactly that – information.

Information about what you're *thinking*.

Without thoughts there would be no feeling. You cannot be happy without having happy thoughts. Ditto angry, sad, miserable, fearful.

If the first domino to topple is that your world is created from thought, the second is the realization that thought is neither real nor permanent. You create it and it swans into your mind where it gets matched up with emotions and – BOOM! – it seems very real and compelling.

'The most difficult thing to learn is something you think you know already.'

Jiddu Krishnamurti

You need to get as far as the third domino. If this one goes, there's a wonderful chain reaction that goes on *and on and on and on and on* for as long as you do. It's this: once you know this stuff, and you give your mind the opportunity, it will self-correct.

Cutting to the chase, here's as deep as we can go …

Your ego – who you *think* you are – needs an identity. That's why it compares you with everyone else. It's a hungry bastard. Insatiably so. Hence why it chases materialism to quench its moreish thirst. Your ego wants you to feel amazing so it's forever trying to shape the external world to make it exactly what you want.

Being aware that your feelings aren't coming from the external world, but from your *thinking* (always, in every situation, forever) means you can give up the chase. Accepting that the world isn't going to shape itself around you and it's never going to be perfect, means you can surrender to what is.

This is not a sign of weakness, it's a sign of wisdom.

You are relinquishing control of a world that is uncontrollable. This doesn't make you powerless. It *gives* you power.

A tremendous weight is lifted when you decide to let go of things that are beyond your control. You decide to accept that sometimes, people won't like you, that often you will fail, that usually you don't have a clue what you're doing and that making it up as you go along is a perfectly acceptable plan.

And Breeeeeathe …

Our research has uncovered an amazing statistic; something the media fails to report. The biggest killer in the UK, bigger than road accidents, cancer, heart attacks, falling off ladders and tripping over squirrels put together.

'Not breathing.' It's literally the number one killer in the UK and the biggest cause of death across the world. It's a scandal. Yet the media fails to report it.

So breathe. And keep breathing. It's really rather important.

If it's so important, maybe we should spend a paragraph on it.

Our advice: Spend 3 minutes breathing well, five times a day.

Here's how. Sit with feet on ground and straight back. Wear a small smile and your clothes, obviously. (Meditating while naked still works, but it's embarrassing if your kids come in.) Close your eyes. Breathe in through your nose for 5 seconds, hold it for 6 seconds and out through your mouth for 7.

Easy enough to remember: 5 in, 6 hold, 7 out.

Here's another. It's quick and easy, just three breaths long. Make them good breaths.

Big breath in.

First, breathe out while you consider how you feel right now.

Big breath in again.

Second out-breath is gratitude, what have you got to be grateful for right now?

Big breath in again.

And your third breath out is what state do you want to be in?
Consider and choose an attitude that will work for you going
forward.

BOOM! You're back in the game.

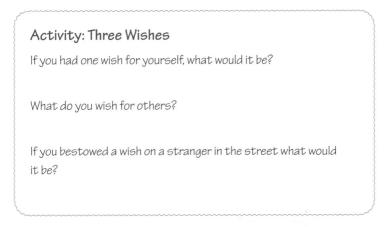

Activity: Three Wishes

If you had one wish for yourself, what would it be?

What do you wish for others?

If you bestowed a wish on a stranger in the street what would
it be?

Now and Then

Here's what we're about to tell you. Let it sink in because we're
coming back to it, via the scenic route.

*You're built for the reality of the present moment. When the
future arrives, IT will be the present moment. The reality you're
built for is here and now.*

A lot is written about 'now'. And by 'now' we mean the present
moment. The only moment. The omnipresent. The only thing that
is constant in your life.

'Now' is a really big deal.

Here's the thing, the outside world is very good at making you
unsettled with your present moment. You're fooled into rushing

through *this* moment because you can sniff the dangling carrot of there being a better moment just around the corner.

The gaping hole in the whole of life is that the better moment, the carroty one, isn't in the future. When you experience it, it will also be your present moment. And, guess what, the carrot has moved to a future moment.

And thus is life. The result is that we're rushing through our moments without ever stopping to register that *this moment is your life.*

Hence the rise of the mindfulness movement, a befriending of the present moment. A call for everyone to slow down, to stop, look and listen out for the wonder of this 'now', on the understanding it's the only one you ever have.

> 'They told me to get a grip on myself, but I'm very slippery, and I got away.'
> *Ashleigh Brilliant*

This is deep shit. But we've included it because we're in deep shit – rushing, musterbating, bemoaning our moments, trying to get somewhere else. We're living life fast, but are we living it well?

And despite all that's been written on mindfulness, we have a soft spot for 'then'.

A happy 'now' can be created by casting your mind back to some wonderful 'thens'.

The past has passed, but that doesn't mean it's gone. The sands of time may have trickled by, but they still exist as something that has tangibly been, occurred, influenced and informed our everyday contemporary living, doing and being.

Just because you're not actually in the moment, doesn't change the fact that it happened, or diminish its worth.

So rather than viewing our bygones as emotional baggage, acned skins to be shed, then why not put them to good use? By all means be selective and travel lightly, but don't throw out the good with the bad in an attempt to pretend that what's gone before has not.

It's possible to reconnect with happy 'present moments' that happened way back. Happy memories act like mental time travel. It's perfectly possible for your happy *thens* to become a rollicking good *now.*

Which is where experiences come to the fore. The top 1000 happiest moments of your entire life are experiences. Moments spent with people you love. In these moments you weren't thinking about happiness, you were experiencing it. These are the moments you were busy laughing through a mouthful of custard creams.

You are testament to the fact that your great, great, great grandparents existed. You are real, living human history. Time doesn't actually change things, rather it's 'things' that change over time. We do things, acquire things and reflect upon things to help put things into perspective. Time doesn't change, people do. Your past shapes you, engulfs you, but that doesn't mean it has to be suffocating. Ignoring what's gone before is ultimately counterproductive; acknowledging your previous enables future growth from firm foundations.

It's never too late to take charge of your yesterdays.

Our mindfulness solutions to living a calmer and happier life are threefold:

> First, bring your attention to the good things. Suck them up. Let some of your best *thens* hitchhike along your timeline to become wonderful *nows.*
>
> Second, rejoice in all the horrible things that haven't happened (we know you're still struggling with that concept but hang in there, it gets stronger with time).

Third, let go. Stop trying to hang on to good experiences. Clinging to them is a sign of desperation.

Relax in the knowledge that the moment will pass – but that another one is already buffering.

Dem Bones, Dem Bones

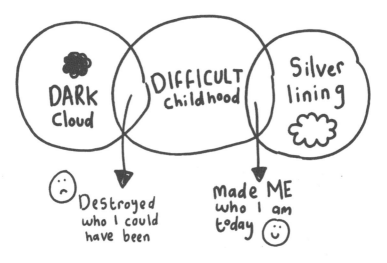

Acknowledge the past. Embrace it. Use it wisely and be selective. But don't live in it.

In all likelihood, the good times vastly outweigh the bad, yet you've somehow been distracted by pop-up skeletons. Errors, misjudgements, violations, deaths, illnesses, mistakes. The bastards are dancing in your cupboard, celebrating hassles, mistakes, failures, misjudgements and disasters from all your yesteryears.

Let the skeletons out.

Then dance with the bastards until they're worn out.

Bouncebackability Dozen

Here's a summary of this chapter. On reflection, some of them are things to do, but most are reminders of things that just are.

We've deliberately sought ideas that are new, different, refreshing, wise, bonkers – but all have positive intent.

Remember, the context of this chapter is that life can be tough. Sometimes it's downright unfair. Cruel even. In the end, the only way you can appreciate your progress is to stand on the edge of the hole you've climbed out of, look down inside it, and smile fondly at the bloody claw prints that marked your journey up the walls.

Here's the most eclectic summary in the history of personal development; our #Bouncebackability12:

1. Nobody knows what they're doing. Congratulations, you're normal. YOU ARE ENOUGH!
2. Embrace your ordinary magic. Time really does heal.
3. It's okay to be a sidekick. Remember those little spuds. They're epic.
4. *Kintsugi*, the golden glue. *Wabi-sabi*, nothing is perfect. You are flawed beauty.
5. Forgiveness, letting go, moving on; these aren't signs of weakness. They're signs of tremendous strength and wisdom.

6. It's too exhausting to give a fuck about everything. Thin your fucks down to a manageable level.

7. ABCDE. Most get as far as Adversity, Belief and Consequence. D asks you to Dispute the belief. Disprove it, even. This gets you to Energy. A solution.

8. Gav stretched it to 'F'. *Fun.* Remember, if all else fails, draw an apple.

9. Shine from the inside out. You are *feeling* your thinking. Your feelings aren't coming from the outside world. They're coming from your thinking. Always. No exceptions. Not ever.

10. And *breeeeeathe* ... keep breathing. It's super important.

11. Become besties with 'now'. This moment, right here, is the only one you ever get.

12. Dance with your skeletons. Lambada them. Wear the bastards out. Floss 'em to death.

Part 10
H^4[NO]R

There's another type of happiness that scientists never talk about. It's not got a silly name like hedonism, eudaimonia or altruism.

It's called 'happiness for no reason' and we've decided to write it as a stupidly complicated and totally meaningless scientific formula to give it some credibility: $H^4[No]R$.

> 'Sucking at something is the first step to becoming sorta good at something.'
>
> *Jake, Adventure Time*

'Happiness for no reason' is the very best sort. No sex, drugs or rock 'n' roll required. Although cake helps.

fuck me, that's a thing of beauty!

Here's our delirious dozen, top tips, happiness hacks, that will help you engage with the gift of life. Commit to them. That way, when the fat lady eventually sings, you'll be sure you go with a satisfied smile of an adventure fully lived.

1. Hug your dog and your partner; not necessarily in that order or at the same time. If all else fails, just try and live up to being the person your dog thinks you are.

2. Listen to your favourite music. Make music. Go to watch people perform music. Sing if you can and most definitely sing if you can't. Sing like you're in the shower.

3. Go outside every day, whatever the weather. Whether or not. Weather the storms, bathe in the sunlight and the moonlight, break the crystallized dew on patchwork autumnal leaves. Soak yourself, and enjoy getting warm and dry. Wear your wellies in the summer.

4. Camp out in your back garden. Nice summer's evening, no tent necessary. Under the stars. Watch the universe shine. You are made of that! [Note, if it's raining, camping out in your lounge is acceptable.]

5. Interact with real people. Some will make you smile, others will make you seek out those that make you smile. Take a moment to listen; think, feel, relate and respond. Then move on, all the richer for that interaction.

6. Remember that the world may be burdened, but you do not have to be its perennial Sherpa. Travel lightly and experience, rather than toiling heavily under creeping despair. The good things are there, and the existence of the bad further elevates the good.

7. Don't think too much. There aren't answers for everything, so it's probably just worth accepting. By all means be inquisitive and certainly seek more than hide, but don't be surprised by the lack of answers. After all, if we knew

everything there is to know, if there was no mystery, we'd be bereft of magic. Everyone needs a little magic and mystery.

8. Don't procrastinate. There is never a good time, but if you're consciously considering when that time might be, as a rule of thumb – it's now. Heed the advice you would give to your friends and act rather than detract, enthuse rather than excuse. Universally, people's biggest regret the world over is regret. If you go out on a limb with your wits about you, then you'll more than likely land on your feet.

9. Eat more of the things that are good for you and some of those that are bad for you. Enjoy them both in moderation. Science will, no doubt, prove or disprove which is indeed which, long after you're gone, so in the meantime: savour culinary pleasures. And cola bottles.

10. Remember that new technology is only temporary; it will soon be old technology. Enjoy the gadgets and gizmos yet don't be distracted by the race to own the latest reincarnation.

11. See everything with a fresh pair of eyes. When you go to work, imagine it's your first day. Be wide-eyed and anticipatory. Greet your family as though you've been away for 6 months. Look at a tree and imagine it's the first time you've ever seen a tree. *Fuck me, that's a thing of beauty. And you say it breathes out oxygen so I can breathe it in? Beautiful and clever. A miracle, for sure.*

12. Rise above mediocrity by doing everything a little bit better than you have to. Remember, there's hardly any traffic on the extra mile.

Part 11

THEY THINK IT'S ALL OVER

Dead or Alive?

There are two types of time in our lives: dead time, when people are passive and waiting, and alive time, when people are learning and thriving and utilizing every second. Every moment presents this choice.

> 'The legend part is easy. It's the living that's hard.'
> *Keith Richards*

4000 weeks. There's only one date that really matters – the last page on the calendar. And when that page comes, when the last date is crossed off, it's over. But it's not all over yet – there's not even people on the pitch.

So alive time or dead time. Which will it be?

Zest. We were keen to pen something that helps you squeeze the max out of your work, relationships and life. But also your time zones; your past, present and future; let's get every last drop of happiness out of those as well.

Way back on page 13, we started with a poem, so let's end with something equally poetic. There's a beautiful song lyric that Supertramp's Roger Hodgson wouldn't allow us to use.

Thanks Roj.

To paraphrase the world-class lyric that we're banned from using, 'The Logical Song' is about when Roger was young, it seemed that life was so wonderful. A miracle! Indeed, it was beautiful and magical.

He sings about the birds in the trees, singing so happily. And joyfully.

And then they sent Roj away to God-knows where. He doesn't specify. But wherever it was, they taught him how to be sensible, logical, responsible. Practical and intellectual. They also showed him how to be cynical. Presumably cynical enough to not let authors quote his exact song lyrics in a book?

We can only give you the gist of the lyric. We have to watch what we say or you'll be calling us radical, liberal, fanatical. *Or criminal!*

It's worth Googling the exact wordage because Roger's spot on with every single line. There are times when the world's asleep. The questions do run deep. It is absurd.

And *Zest* has been about helping answer the question, *please tell me who I am?*

Who Wants to Live Forever?

UK life expectancy is 82.9 years for women and 79.2 for men.

Throughout the book we've been simplifying it to 4000 weeks. You might get a few more, you might get fewer but, on average, you'll be knocking about for around 4000. And yet we have the capacity to go way beyond the average. My lazy Google search reveals that the oldest person ever was a French lady, Jeanne Calment, who zimmered her way to 122. Henry Allingham is the oldest British man in history, tipping the longevity scales at 113 and a bit.

> 'Play for the name on the front of the jersey and they'll remember the name on the back.'
>
> *Tony Adams, Arsenal FC*

But here's the thing. If you Google the longevity league table, you'll notice a lot of Japanese in the list of the world's oldest people. In fact, almost a third of the oldest people who've ever lived are from Japan.

So what the heck's going on over there?

If you look really closely, the Okinawa postcode is where the super-centenarians live.

Here are three Okinawan habits, in no particular order …

They tend to move naturally. Over here we tend to compensate for our sedentary lifestyles with a mad 40 minutes at the gym, whereas the Okinawans cycle or walk. Even in old age, the Japanese will get out and about on foot. In the fresh air.

Is that beyond obvious enough for you?

Second, they live by the philosophy of hara hachi bu, the direct translation of which is 'eat until your belly is 8 tenths full'. In plain simple English it means 'stop eating before it hurts' or even simpler 'stop stuffing your face'. That deep pan meat feast pizza with a crust filled with sausages – you don't need to order it. And if you do order it, it's okay to leave some.

And third, they take pride in belonging to a community and/or extended family. The younger ones have an inbuilt sense of moral responsibility to take care of their elders so grandma and grandad will live with the family. Great-grandma too, seeing she's going to be around till she's 125! Crucially, the elderly aren't viewed as doddery old idiots, they're respected for the wisdom that comes from having lived so many decades.

Plus, they're really useful because they can cycle to the shops.

Grey Matter Matters

The problem with modernity is that the medical profession has become very adept at keeping us alive, often well past our 'best before' date. New knees and hips can be slotted into place. Maybe a kidney. Hearts can be triple bypassed or electronically paced. Cancers can be irradiated. Tumours removed. Basically, even if your big end's gone, the doctors can put you a new one in.

Medical science is amazing, so why did we prefix that paragraph with the word 'problem'?

Because you and I know that sometimes the mind can't keep up. If your brain is programmed to last 75 years and your body parts allow you to get to 120, then you've got a problem. Everyone reading this book will have a relative or friend whose mind is deteriorating.

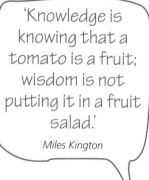

'Knowledge is knowing that a tomato is a fruit; wisdom is not putting it in a fruit salad.'

Miles Kington

At the time of writing, there's no wonder drug that gives you your mind back.

So here's our final tried and academically tested thought; if you're planning on living for more than 4000 weeks (which we know you are) then you need to prep your grey matter. There's nothing the medical profession can do about what's going on between your ears so you need to take care of your brain cells. Starting NOW!

Look after these...

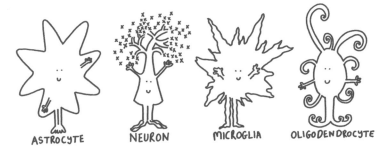

ASTROCYTE   NEURON   MICROGLIA   OLIGODENDROCYTE

also known as your brain cells!

Your grey matter *really* matters! We've listed what's good and bad for your brain, side by side, so it's easy to compare and contrast.

Good for your brain cells	Bad for your brain cells
Positivity. It keeps those neurons firing	Negativity. Slows everything down
Food with natural colour; blueberries, avos, broccoli, wild salmon	Grey or beige food. Trans saturated fat (pies, sausage rolls, fried food, etc.)
Tea (with no sugar)	Fizzy pop. Energy drinks. The immediate hit is negated by the long-term lull
Exercise	Sitting
Purpose. A reason for getting out of bed	Lack of purpose. No reason for getting out of bed
Alcohol (Moderate. An occasional glass of red, for example)	Alcohol (excessive)

(continued)

Good for your brain cells	Bad for your brain cells
'Hara hachi bu' (eat moderately)	Overeating (hence morbid obesity which leads to a sedentary lifestyle. Once you can't be arsed to move from the sofa, you're doomed)
Natural light	Stuck indoors
Sleep	Lack of sleep
Getting a dog (forces you to go walkies)	Pet tortoise (distinct lack of walkies)
Being with people	Isolation. Loneliness
Sunshine. Being outdoors	Darkness. Being indoors
De-stressing (e.g. sex)	Chronic stress
Cannaboids (e.g. marijuana)	Cocaine

Check the lists and decide which looks like the best night out? To be fair, they both have good bits and bad bits. Lessons for me? Cut the negativity, beige food and sitting. Get out more, generate more positive thoughts and book a trip to Amsterdam.

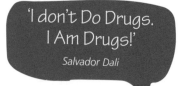

'I don't Do Drugs. I Am Drugs!'

Salvador Dali

We're not expecting you to give the Okinawans a run for their money. Sure, applying the laws of *Zest* can add a few more years to your life but if you've gotten this deeply into our book you'll have realized it's MUCH bigger than that.

It's about adding more life to your years.

Life: You're 'It'

Let's fast-forward to your ancient years, a life beyond 4000 weeks. Imagine the world. It's the same as now, but a whole lot faster and a whole lot lonelier. I doubt there will be much eye contact?

> 'The evidence is in, and you are the verdict.'
> *Anne Lamott*

Living amongst us are a chosen few. They are special, by any measure. On the scale of special, they're not just in the red, they're in the red, orange, yellow, green, blue, indigo, violet; the whole spectrum. And this is one spectrum we should all be on.

You are one of them.

Sometimes they go about their everyday business mingling amongst us unseen, unheard, incognito. At others, you cannot fail to notice them; they stop you dead in your tracks, as you gape open-mouthed, eyes-agog at the enormity of what you have just witnessed. You shield your eyes, blinded by the sheer magnitude of unconventional unadulterated audacity. You've encountered those who are made of The Bright Stuff. The *cor!-couture*.

The Bright Stuff defy conventional wisdom and belie expectation. Gosh! Those adorned with yellow corduroy jackets and purple polka-dot cravats, or perhaps orange velour flares and lime-green waistcoats. Definitely not matching. Slightly ill-fitting combinations jar with designer labels. Low-slung Golddigga denims pulled high above the waist prove comfort and ante-fashion can be compatible. Age is no barrier. They go where no one else dares.

They wear what no one else dares.

The Bright Stuff are the twilight of society; wearing their wrinkles well with lines of laughter and ever-present twinkles. Adorned with fantastical combinations of clashing corduroy and vomitus velour, they are the proud, preening peacocks amongst a poppycock of pigeons.

They are the blissfully aware, although it hasn't always been this way. Once upon a time, The Bright Stuff, like the rest of us, supressed the urge to stand out, instead opting to camouflage amongst the masses of mediocrity; an impression of expression, paling amongst insipid suburbia and ill-fitting-in. And then …

They got it. YOU got it! An epiphany. They grew older. And wiser. And with the wisdom of advancing years came an ante-wisdom; the recognition that growing up is not about blending in; that getting older should be about getting bolder and brighter as your individuality comes into sharper focus.

Retirement should be the pinnacle of life – the culmination not so much of a working life, but a life's work. The twilight years should accentuate a glorious diversity of individual choice, quirks, decisions and experiences. Individuality should scream louder at 80 than 40; the further you dance along the yellow brick road and shimmer with the zimmer.

The Bright Stuff get this: they've accrued a lifetime's momentum.

Going out is about going out in style; in a blaze of velour glory.

'I would rather be ashes than dust! I would rather that my spark should burn out in a brilliant blaze than it should be stifled by dry-rot. I would rather be a superb meteor, every atom of me in magnificent glow, than a sleepy and permanent planet. The function of man is to live, not to exist. I shall not waste my days in trying to prolong them. I shall use my time.'

Jack London

It was Mary Poole who said, 'He who laughs, lasts'. And gosh, that's clever.

And true.

The game of life, ain't none of us getting out alive.

But we can get out happy. We can all – every one of us – die young.

Ultimately, your matter doesn't matter. Your imprint will leave barely a trace.

And that's something to celebrate rather than commiserate. You are not burdened, lumbering through life with the world's burgeoning population upon your shoulders, but free. Free, just to be. Despite the end being nigh, it's no bitter end.

Maybe the meaning of life is just that: life. To live, love, inhale and regale before your date with expiry. To inhabit your true self, rather than forever seeking to escape by replicating others. To squeeze every last drop of existence from your briefest history-of-time.

None of us really knows anything for sure, despite what the academics and historians surmise. We can only postulate and hypothesize third-hand, from fossilized remains and galactic echoes of remote supernovas, DNA of the long-since deceased and etchings carved in crumbling red sandstone.

We may not know, but we can feel. *Feeling* is akin to living. To being alive.

And I'm not just talking the regular selection box of emotions of love, hate, blood, sweat, and tears. It's the stuff that falls between: Turkish delight and coffee-creams, the residue of the unspoken and unsaid, the alternative sediment that gathers in unusual places giving life texture and taste.

So?

Shy away from perceived wisdoms and the constraints of convention. Listen to the whispers of your individuality; the moments when the world's illuminated by the twinkles in your eye. Do more of them, for only good can come of them. Personality shines brightly.

Individuality shines even brighter.

Pretoogjes: Dutch.

'Fun eyes'; the twinkling eyes of someone engaging in benign mischief or fun.

Revisit that which resonates. The times and places where you fit; the jigsaw that embraces your jagged edges. Enjoy when you fit in, embrace when you stand out.

Do the things that you know you should and choose some of those that you know you shouldn't. Caution keeps you safe, but can also keep you the same. To experience something different, you must check the desire to keep you in check.

Do the stuff you're not cut out to do. Then you'll really know whether you're cut out to do it. You will surprise yourself.

Make something new, craft something better and don't be defined by what's already in existence. The traditional path has navigated the past, the future may require something quite different. Someone quite different. Someone like you.

Play more, for no reason. H^4[No]R. Happiness does not require a purpose. A purpose, however, is served well by happiness.

If work grinds you down, do everything you can to work out an alternative that works for you. The act of instigating change is often all the change that is needed.

Don't hesitate, you really don't have the time. Your veins course with life and your body pulses with potential, but you must first dismiss the impulse to dismiss. Behind every door of every street resides abundant possibility and opportunity, yet so much remains unrequited and unquenched. Regret is perhaps the only human characteristic that grows stronger as the body grows weaker.

Squeeeeeeze. Squeeze every moment of every day and immerse yourself in the sweet, sticky stuff that bursts forth. Savour the tang and the sharpness. Wake up to the possibilities, for they are absolutely not endless. You will breathe your last breath and that will be that. In the meantime, delight in the world and its bewildering complexities. Don't try to understand it all. Take nothing for granted. Determine to change, and if not change then just determine. Half-measures will sell you short. Hold those close to you closer. Bring them with you on the adventure.

Look to the future with childish glee and unadulterated joy. Do more than just look; craft, create, ignite and excite until you cannot contain yourself any longer.

Life may have given you lemons, but the *Zest* really is up to you.

Choose life.

Juice life.

Live.

Acknowledgements

Will would like to thank Teddy, Martha and Henry for their daringly happy contribution. And Mike Hussey, brimming with the Bright Stuff.

Gav would like to thank all the team at Tree of Knowledge (www.treeof.com) for their continued support. And of course the hottest band in the world, KISS.

Andy would like to tug his forelock to the team at Art of Brilliance for continuing to live on the edges of possibility. Our stated aim *'to rid the world of shit training'* is taking longer than anticipated but we're making good inroads.

There's a host of academic and creative heroes too. I'm not a natural academic and, boy, do I swoon at those who are! That'll be the Seligmans, Achors and Dieners of this world. More recently, I've been inspired by the anti-academia of Syd Banks. His principles of mind, thought and consciousness have crept into my recent books, so a huge mention needs to go to Jamie Smart who, for me, is the world's finest exponent of the 3Ps. By a mile.

I'd also like to nod to my fellow authors, Will and Gav. Will, because he's such an effortless wordsmith that it forces me to up my game. And Gav? We did *SHINE* together and, although I'm very proud of my back catalogue, Gav gave me confidence to be more me and (I think?) write in a way that has more impact.

And I'm totally aware that I could never have studied for a PhD or written any books without a wonderful family and self-rearing children.

The writing team

Dr Andy Cope is a happiness researcher, author and learning junkie. He writes for adults and children. Andy also delivers some wicked keynote talks on themes of well-being, resilience, positivity, leadership and human flourishing. He's worked with all sorts of businesses in all parts of the world. Andy's stuff is showcased at www.artofbrilliance.co.uk and www.brilliant.school or you can stalk him on Twitter at @beingbrilliant, Instagram @artofbrilliance and FB artbeingbrilliant.

Gavin Oattes is a once in a lifetime type of human. Think Optimus Prime meets Freddie Mercury meets Mary Poppins. Someone who just simply wants to inspire the world, help others to help themselves and always, *always* put on the best show possible. Award-winning Entrepreneur, Comedian and Author, book him as your keynote speaker and learn just why some of the biggest companies in the world turn to Gav to inspire their people! Find him on Twitter @gavinoattes and at www.gavinoattes.com for more.

Will Hussey is an award-winning best-selling author and keynote speaker, who specializes in making a difference. He encourages people to think, think again and grow. You can check Will out at www.artofbrilliance.co.uk or you can tweet him at @aobrillwill

Index

Q. What do all these things have in common?
Stars. Sun. Moon. People.

A. They all make you feel better when they SHINE!

SHINE

Rediscovering your energy,
happiness & purpose

ANDY COPE & GAVIN OATTES

Find out just how easy it is to boost your energy and increase your motivation. Discover how to break free from 'ordinary' and embrace a life of 'extraordinary.' Figure out how to channel your inner Mary Poppins or Peter Pan. The self-help book that people read again and again.